James McNicol

Remarks on Dr. Samuel Johnson's Journey to the Hebrides

James McNicol

Remarks on Dr. Samuel Johnson's Journey to the Hebrides

ISBN/EAN: 9783337067243

Printed in Europe, USA, Canada, Australia, Japan

Cover: Foto ©Andreas Hilbeck / pixelio.de

More available books at **www.hansebooks.com**

Feb 6. 1871. –

Mr. Ludovick Cameron grandson of the author met in Mull in 1870 - at Knock; called with manuscripts collected by his grandfather in dios montis. Here is his autograph & his directions is
Care of the oriental Bank.

A Cameron

Feb 8th Looked through the collection which is contained in a tin tea chest 10 by 7 by 7 inches. Found the manuscripts of a book and of articles in Magazines signed Hebridean in English

a bit of a Hebrew & English
Vocab'y   a bit of English
old almost illegible —

a lot of small paper books of
a few leaves folded and stitched
by the minister apparently, with
his signature upon them, and
with more recent notes here
and there in newer ink & a
modern hand. These
contain. Gaelic songs by well
known bards such as those
which are in Mackenzie's beauties
of Gaelic Poetry; The Owl —
and a lot of Fenian ballads &c
like those which were printed
by Gillies in 1786. There is
~~but~~ one fragment of Gaelic
stuff like that of 1807 &
1786. Macdubh & that

class. The result of this enquiry is that the author was justified in saying that he recognised genuine Gaelic ossianic poetry in MacPherson's English which was known to him. He names some of the poems which he recognised and here they are amongst his manuscripts.

But if he had the Gaelic of 1807 to compare with his Gaelic of 1751. Or other dates he would have seen the difference as I do. — Now MacNicol had Ossianic

Feb. 13. Finished sorting the manuscripts and put all the Ossian's bits together in one envelope, No 11. There 29 of them enough to make a small Volume.

May 9/1876. Mr. Roderick Cameron called, and pointed out some errors in Leabhar na Féinne Page 15. Introduction. That book contains an account of MacNicol's manuscript above referred to, and the ballads themselves printed from the manuscript 1872 by
J. F. Campbell

REMARKS

ON

Dr. SAMUEL JOHNSON's

JOURNEY to the HEBRIDES

REMARKS

ON

Dr. SAMUEL JOHNSON's

JOURNEY to the HEBRIDES;

IN WHICH ARE CONTAINED,

OBSERVATIONS on the ANTIQUITIES, LANGUAGE, GENIUS, and MANNERS of the HIGHLANDERS of SCOTLAND.

BY

The Rev. DONALD M'NICOL, A. M.
Minifter of LISMORE in ARGYLESHIRE.

Old Men and *Travellers* LIE by Authority.
RAY's Proverbs.

LONDON:
PRINTED FOR T. CADELL, IN THE STRAND.
M.DCC.LXXIX.

TO

HUGH SETON, Esq.

OF APPIN,

THE FOLLOWING SHEETS

ARE

WITH GREAT RESPECT

INSCRIBED

BY

THE AUTHOR.

ADVERTISEMENT.

THE following Sheets were written soon after Dr. Johnson's "Journey to the Hebrides" was printed. But as the writer had never made his appearance at the bar of the Public, he was unwilling to enter the lifts, with such a *powerful* antagonist, without previously consulting a few learned friends. The distance of those friends made it difficult to procure their opinion, without some trouble and a great loss of time: besides, the Author was not so fond of his work as to be very anxious about its publication.

dom extend beyond the circle of their private acquaintance, it is from the latter only that we can expect a more public and particular information relative to foreign parts. Some ingenious and valuable productions of this kind have lately made their appearance; and when a man communicates, with candour and fidelity, what he has seen in other countries, he cannot render a more agreeable or useful service to his own.

By such faithful portraits of men and manners, we are presented with a view of the world around us, as it really is. Our Author, like a trusty guide, conducts us through the scenes he describes, and makes us acquainted with the inhabitants; and thus we reap all the pleasures and advantages of travel, without the inconveniencies attending it. There is no country so contemptible as not to furnish some things that may please, nor is any arrived to that degree

degree of perfection as to afford no matter of diflike. When, therefore, no falfe colouring is ufed, to diminifh what is commendable, or magnify defects, we often find reafon to give up much of our fuppofed fuperiority over other nations. Hence our candour increafes with our knowledge of mankind, and we get rid of the folly of prejudice and felf-conceit; which is equally ridiculous in a people as individuals, and equally an obftacle to improvement.

It were to be wifhed that the Treatife, which is the fubject of the following fheets, had been formed on fuch a plan as has been now mentioned, as it would be a much more agreeable tafk to commend than cenfure it. But it will appear, from the fequel, how far its author has acquitted himfelf with that candour which could inform the curious, or undeceive the prejudiced.

When it was known, about two years ago, that Dr. Samuel Johnson, a man of some reputation for letters, had undertaken a tour through Scotland, it was naturally enough expected, that one of his contemplative turn would, some time or other, give a public account of his journey. His early prejudices against the country were sufficiently known; but every one expected a fair, if not a flattering, representation, from the narrative of grey hairs. But there was another circumstance which promised a collateral security for the Doctor's fair dealing. Mr. Pennant, and other gentlemen of abilities and integrity, had made the same tour before him, and, like men of liberal sentiments, spoke respectfully of the Scotch nation. It was thought, therefore, that this, if nothing else, would prove a check on his prepossessions, and make him extremely cautious, were it only for his own sake, how he contradicted such respectable authorities.

Neither

Neither of these considerations, however, had any weight. The Doctor hated Scotland; that was the *master-passion*, and it scorned all restraints. He seems to have set out with a design to give a distorted representation of every thing he saw on the north side of the Tweed; and it is but doing him justice to acknowledge, that he has not failed in the execution.

But consistency has not always been attended to in the course of his narration. He differs no more from other travellers, than he often does from himself, denying at one time what he has asserted at another, as prejudice, or a more generous passion, happened, by turns, to prevail; which, to say no worse, is but an aukward situation for a man who makes any pretensions to be believed.

At the same time I am not so partial to my country, as to say that Dr. Johnson is always in the wrong when he finds fault.

On the contrary, I am ready to allow him, as, I believe, will every Scotchman, that the road through the mountains, from Fort Auguſtus to Glenelg, is not quite ſo ſmooth as that between London and Bath; and that he could not find, in the huts or cottages at *Anoch* and *Glenſheals*, the ſame luxuries and accommodations as in the inns on an Engliſh poſt-road. In theſe, and ſuch like remarks, the Doctor's veracity muſt certainly remain unimpeached. But the bare merit of telling truth will not always atone for a want of candour in the intention. In the more remote and unfrequented parts of a country, little refinement is to be expected; it is, therefore, no leſs frivolous to examine them with too critical an eye, than diſingenuous to exhibit them as ſpecimens of the reſt. This, however, has been too much the practice with Dr. Johnſon, in his account of Scotland; every trifling defect is eagerly brought forward, while the more perfect parts of the piece

piece are as carefully kept out of view. If other travellers were to proceed on the fame plan, what nation in Europe but might be made to appear ridiculous?

The objects of any moment, which have been chiefly diftinguifhed by that *odium* which Dr. Johnfon bears to every thing that is Scotch, feem to be—the Poems of Offian,—the whole Gallic language,—our feminaries of learning,—the Reformation,—and the veracity of all Scotch, and particularly Highland narration. The utter extinction of the two former feems to have been the principal motive of his journey to the North. To pave the way for this favourite purpofe, and being aware that the influence of tradition, to which all ages and nations have ever paid fome regard in matters of remote antiquity, muft be removed, he refolves *point blank* to deny the validity of all Scotch, and particularly Highland narration. This he employs all his art to perfuade the Public is always vague and fabulous, and deferves no manner of credit, except when it proves unfavourable to the country; then, indeed, it is deemed altogether infallible, and is adduced by himfelf, upon all occafions, in proof of what he afferts. But this is a mode of reafoning with which the world has been totally unacquainted before the Doctor's days.

The Poems of Offian were no fooner made known to the Public, though ftript of their native ancient garb, than they became the delight and admiration of the learned over all Europe. Dr. Johnfon, perhaps, was the only man, of any pretenfions to be ranked in that clafs, who chofe to diffent from the general voice. The moment he heard of the publication and fame of thofe Poems, he declared them fpurious, without waiting for the common formality of a perufal. His cynical difpofition inftantly took

took the alarm; and that, aided by his prejudices, would not suffer him to admit that a composition of such acknowledged merit could originate from a country which, because he hated, he always affected to despise.

But what is the consequence of this hasty and absurd declaration? After all that has been said upon the subject, the Poems must still be considered as the production either of Ossian or Mr. Macpherson. Dr. Johnson does not vouchsafe to tell us who else was the author; and consequently the national claim remains perfectly entire. In labouring to deny their antiquity, therefore, the Doctor only plucks the wreath of ages from the tomb of the ancient bard, to adorn the brow of the modern Caledonian. For the moment Mr. Macpherson ceases to be admitted as a translator, he instantly acquires a title to the original.—This consequence is unavoidable, though it is not to
be

be supposed Dr. Johnson intended it. Naturally pompous and vain, and ridiculously ambitious of an exclusive reputation in letters, it can hardly be believed that he would voluntarily bestow so envied a compliment on a young candidate for fame, who had already, in other respects, made a discovery of talents sufficient to alarm his own pride: but we often derive from the folly of some men, more than we claim from their justice.

From the first appearance of Ossian's Poems in public, we may date the origin of Dr. Johnson's intended tour to Scotland; whatever he may pretend to tell us, in the beginning of his narration. There are many circumstances to justify this opinion; among which a material one is, that a gentleman of undobted honour and veracity, who happened to be at London soon after that period, informed me upon his return to the country, that Caledonia might,

some

some day, look for an unfriendly visit from the Doctor. So little able was he, it seems, to conceal his ill-humour on that occasion, that it became the subject of common discourse; and the event has fully verified what was predicted as the consequence.

In the year 1773 he accomplished his purpose; and sometime in the year following he published an account of his journey, which plainly shews the spirit with which it was undertaken. All men have their prejudices more or less, nor are the best always without them; but so sturdy an instance as this is hardly to be met with. It is without example, in any attempt of the like kind that has gone before it; and it is to be hoped, for the sake of truth and the credit of human nature, it will furnish none to such as may come after.

As, in refuting the misrepresentations and detecting the inconsistencies of Dr. Johnson,

Johnson, it may sometimes be found necessary to draw a comparison between the north and the south side of the Tweed, it is proper to premise here, that this shall always be done, without the least intention to reflect on the English nation. My mind was perfectly free from the narrowness of national prejudice before this occasion; and I am not yet sufficiently provoked, by the Doctor's injustice to my country, to retaliate against his. To illustrate the subject by similar instances, is my only aim; as then, like objects brought nearer to the eye, observations, when applied more immediately to ourselves, will strike more forcibly.—This much, I hope, will suffice as an apology with every candid Englishman. And as to some people among ourselves, who easily give up many points of national honour, they are chiefly upstarts in the world; a set of men, who, in all countries, are apt to make light of

distinctions

diftinctions from which their own obfcurity excludes them.

My firft intention was to write what I had to fay on this fubject in the form of an Effay. Upon farther confideration, however, the method I have now adopted appeared the moft eligible; as, by citing the Doctor's own words, the Public will be the better enabled to judge what juftice is done to his meaning. This plan, on account of the frequent interruptions, may not, perhaps, render the performance fo entertaining to fome readers; but it gives an opportunity for a more clofe inveftigation, and to fuch as are not poffeffed of the Doctor's book, it will, in a great meafure, fupply its place.

That the reader may not be difappointed, I muft tell him before-hand, that he is not to expect, in the following fheets, what Dr. Johnfon calls " *ornamental fplendors.*" Impartiality

partiality of obfervation fhall be more attended to than elegance of diction; and if I appear fometimes fevere, the Doctor fhall have no reafon to fay I am unjuft. He is to be tried all along by his own evidence; and, therefore, he cannot complain, if, " out of his own mouth, he is condemned."

Dr. Johnfon informs us, that he fet out from Edinburgh, upon his intended peregrination, the 18th of Auguft 1773. This muft undoubtedly appear an uncommon feafon of the year for an old frail inhabitant of London to undertake a journey to the Hebrides, if he propofed the tour fhould prove agreeable to himfelf, or amufing to the Public. Moft other travellers make choice of the fummer months, when the countries through which they pafs are feen to moft advantage; and as the Doctor acknowledges he had been hitherto but little out of the metropolis, one fhould think he would have wifhed to have made the moft

of

of his journey. But it was not beauties the Doctor went to find out in Scotland, but defects; and for the northern situation of the Hebrides, the advanced time of the year suited his purpose best.

He passes over the city of *Edinburgh* almost without notice; though surely its magnificent castle, its palace, and many stately buildings, both public and private, were not unworthy of a slight touch, at least, from the Doctor's pencil. Little, therefore, is to be expected from a man who would turn his back on the capital with a supercilious silence. But, indeed, he is commonly very sparing of his remarks where there is any thing that merits attention; though we find he has always enough to say where none but himself could find matter of observation.

In page 3d, his account of the *island* of *Inch Keith* is trifling and contradictory.

He

He represents it as a barren rock where there formerly was a fort; and yet he tells us again, that it was never intended for a place of strength, and that a "herd of cows grazes annually upon it in the summer." But a *fort* without *strength* is surely something *new*, and grazing for cattle a most *uncommon mark* of barrenness.

Before the Doctor dismisses this *wonderful* spot, which he has made something and nothing all in a breath,—he amuses himself with thinking "on the different appearance that it would have made, if it had been placed at the same distance from London;" and then he adds, with an air of exultation, "with what emulation of price a few rocky acres would have been purchased, and with what expensive industry they would have been cultivated and adorned."

The censure implied in the above passage is obvious; but, to give it effect, the Doctor ought

ought first to determine whether Inch Keith is not still a royal property. Should that be found to be the case, no *emulation of price* could purchase it; and consequently the citizens of Edinburgh are not to be blamed for not *cultivating* and *adorning* what they cannot make their own.

But this consideration set apart, let me ask the Doctor, Whether the Londoners have shewn themselves so very deserving of the *ranting* compliment he pays them? If I am not misinformed, there are, at this present moment, even in the very heart of the cities of London and Westminster, many extensive spots of ground, which exhibit at once the most miserable marks of desolation, and proofs of neglect. Instead of being *cultivated* and *adorned*, these are represented as dangerous to the passenger, and loathsome to the view. What then are we to think of this boasted *emulation* to purchase, this *industry* to improve? Is it

C   very

very credible, that a people fhould go fuch *expenfive* lengths for an agreeable fituation without their walls, who permit the vileft finks of filth and corruption to incommode and difgrace their ftreets?

The Doctor fays, he difcovered no woods in his way towards Cowpar. This may be true, as the Doctor's optics, I am told, are none of the beft. But furely the fine extenfive plantations of the Earl of Leven's eftate, and not very diftant from the public road, could not well have efcaped the notice of any other paffenger. He then tells us, that " a tree is as great a curiofity in Scotland, as a horfe at Venice."—I cannot decide upon the merits of this affertion, as I am not acquainted with the numbers of the Venetian cavalry. But, whatever the Doctor may infinuate about the prefent fcarcity of trees in Scotland, we are much deceived by fame, if a very near anceftor of his, who was a native of that country,

did

did not find to his coft, that a *tree* was not quite fuch a rarity in *his* days.

It is allowed, indeed, he might pafs through fome parts of Scotland where there are not many trees; as, I believe, is the cafe in England, and moft other countries. But as he is fo very careful in defcribing the nakednefs of the country where trees were not, he ought to have had the candour likewife to inform us where they were.

Such, however, as are defirous of fatiffaction on this head, may confult Mr. *Pennant*'s Tour, and they will find a very different account of the matter from that given by the Doctor. That gentleman found abundance of woods, and even *trees*, in different parts of the country, if thofe of twelve and fifteen feet in circumference may deferve that name. But *he* travelled with his judgment *unbiaffed*, and his eyes open;

open; two circumstances in which he differed very materially from Dr. Johnson, and which, rather somewhat unluckily for the latter, has occasioned such a frequent difference in their accounts.

As the Doctor arrived at *St. Andrews* at two in the morning, it is pleasant enough to hear him say, " Though we were yet in the most populous part of Scotland, and at so small a distance from the capital, we met few passengers."—Few people, I believe, would complain of this circumstance, at the *same* hours, and at so *small* a distance from the English capital. But it is pretty evident, that the Doctor meant nothing less than a compliment to the Scots, for the security with which he performed this nocturnal expedition.

But the night is the natural season for rest; and that being considered, it effectually takes the *sting* from the above *silly* remark.

remark. What man in his senses would expect to find crowded roads at midnight? Or what man of common honesty would be bold enough to assert, that there were few or no trees in Fife, because forsooth they were not to be seen in the dark?

He says (page 7), that there is hardly so much of the *cathedral* of St. Andrews remaining "as to exhibit, even to an artist, a sufficient specimen of the architecture."— I am at a loss to know what he means by a *sufficient specimen*, if a great part of one of the side-walls, with a spire at each end, and the main entry entire, are not *sufficient* for the purpose he mentions: for all these still remain in spite of *Knox's reformation*, as he sarcastically expresses it.

In 1543, a bill was passed in the parliament of Scotland, granting leave to the people to read the scriptures in the vulgar tongues; and this bill was notified to the Public,

Public, by a proclamation from the regent. He even went so far as to desire Sir Ralph Sadler, the English ambassador, to send for English bibles from London. As this deed, therefore, had the sanction of the regent and parliament, let the world judge of the candour of the man who calls it *Knox's reformation.*

Page 8th.—He mentions the miserable but just fate of cardinal *Beatoune,* in such a manner as might make it be thought to have proceeded from the religious animosities of those times; for he says, " that he was murdered by the ruffians of reformation." But it is well known to such as are conversant in the history of that period, that it was not for his religion that this pest of society was brought to an untimely end. His numberless cruelties and oppressions had raised him many enemies among all ranks of people; and in particular there was an old quarrel between him

him and *Norman Lefly*, fon to the Earl of Rothes, who was the principal agent in ridding the world of a monfter, who ought rather to have fallen by the hand of public juftice.

But while our Author condemns this act with fo much *malignant* acrimony, he takes care, with his ufual candour, to conceal from his reader the more to be lamented fate of the amiable *Wifhart*; who but a few days before, and that for confcience fake alone, was condemned to the flames, and fuffered accordingly, by one of the many barbarous decrees of the Doctor's *favourite* cardinal, though there was an exprefs order from the regent to the contrary. If this was not *murder* with a vengeance, I fhould be glad to know its proper name. But as it was perpetrated under the fanction of a *popifh* judicatory, the Doctor may, perhaps, foften perfecution into juftice, and roundly affirm that

the

the *devoted* Wishart deserved no mercy, for the unpardonable crime, according to him, of being one of the *ruffians of reformation*. He seems, indeed, to have a good deal of the *old leaven* in his composition; and whatever may be his notions of civil liberty, he shews himself, upon most occasions, to be no great friend to *that of* conscience.

Towards the bottom of the same page, he asserts, that all the civilization introduced into Scotland, is entirely owing to our trade and intercourse with England.—It is but too common with English writers to speak contemptuously, of other countries, and arrogate very largely to their own; and what with national vanity on the one hand, and national prejudice on the other, the Doctor has, in this instance, either suffered himself to be betrayed into a most gross and wilful misrepresentation, or he discovers an amazing ignorance of

the

the history of Europe. This *miracle* of knowledge did not know, or is willing to forget, that, long before the period he alludes to, we had an intercourse of many centuries with France; a nation as *polite*, at least, as *England*, and, perhaps, full as ready to do justice to the characters of their neighbours.

Our first league with France was in the reign of Charlemagne, in 792, signed by that monarch, and afterwards by our king Achaius, at *Inverlochoy*. Charles the Great was so fond of ennobling France, not only by arms but by arts, that he sent for learned men from Scotland, says Buchanan, to read philosophy, in Greek and Latin, at Paris. He himself had for his preceptor, Johannes Scotus, or Albinus, a man eminent for learning.

Many other Scots went over about that time, to instruct the inhabitants about the Rhine

Rhine in the doctrines of Christianity; which they did with such success, that the people built monasteries in many places. The Germans paid such a respect to their memories, that, even in Buchanan's time, Scotchmen were made governors of those monasteries.

From the time of Achaius to the Union, our alliance with France continued. A complete catalogue of all those treaties, with an English translation, was published in 1751; to which I refer the Doctor, to convince him, that we had some importance as a nation, before we had any connection with his country. There he will see the uncommon privileges we enjoyed in France:—That we were entrusted with the highest offices, civil, military, and ecclesiastical:—That we were complimented with all the rights and franchises of native subjects, which we possess to this day:—And that we were distinguished by the fingular honour of acting as lifeguards to the French kings; a truft, one would think, not to be conferred on fuch *favages* and *barbarians* as the Doctor would make us.

Our merchants likewife enjoyed the moft uncommon privileges and immunities in France: and many of our nobility and gentlemen obtained extenfive eftates in that kingdom, as rewards for their fignal fervices to the ftate, which the pofterity of moft of them inherit to this day.

There cannot, I think, be a more convincing proof of the entire confidence which the French repofed in the honour and fidelity of the Scots, than their making choice of them for guarding the perfons of their fovereigns. After *Lewis* XII. had fet forth, in terms the moft honourable to our nation, the fervices
which

which the Scots had performed for *Charles* the Seventh, in expelling the English out of France, and reducing the kingdom to his obedience, he adds,—" Since which " reduction, and for the service the Scots " rendered to Charles the Seventh, upon " that occasion, and for the great loyalty " and virtue which he found in them, he " selected 200 of them for the guard of his " person, of whom he made an hundred " *men at arms,* and an hundred *life-guards:* " And the hundred men at arms are the " hundred lances of our ancient ordinances; " and the life-guard men are those of our " guard, who still are near and about our " person."

With respect to the fidelity of the Scots in this honourable station, let us hear the testimony of *Claud Seyfil,* Master of Requests to the same Lewis XII. and afterwards Archbishop of Turin, in the history of that prince; where, speaking of Scotland,

Scotland, he says,—" The French have so
" ancient a friendship and alliance with
" the Scots, that, of 400 men appointed
" for the king's life-guard, there are an
" hundred of the said nation who are the
" nearest to his person, and, in the night,
" keep the keys of the apartment where
" he sleeps. There are, moreover, an
" hundred complete lances, and two hun-
" dred yeomen of the said nation, besides
" several that are dispersed through the
" companies: and for so long a time as
" they have served in *France*, never hath
" there been one of them found, that hath
" committed, or done any fault, against
" the kings or their state; and they make
" use of them as of their own subjects."

The ancient rights and privileges of the Scottish life-guards were very honourable. Here follows a description of the functions and precedence belonging to their company, and especially to the twenty-four
first

firſt guards; to whom the firſt *gendarme* of France being added, they make up the number of twenty-five, commonly called *gardes de manche* (ſleeve guards) who were all Scotch by nation. The Author of the ancient alliance ſays,—" Two of them
" aſſiſt at maſs, ſermon, veſpers, and or-
" dinary meals. On high holidays, at the
" ceremony of the *royal touch*, the erec-
" tion of Knights of the King's order, the
" reception of extraordinary ambaſſadors,
" and the public entries of cities, there
" muſt be ſix of their number next to the
" King's perſon, three on each ſide of his
" Majeſty: and the body of the king muſt
" be carried by theſe only, whereſoever
" ceremony requires; and his effigy muſt
" be attended by them. They have the
" keeping of the keys of the king's lodg-
" ing at night, the keeping of the choir
" of the chapel, the keeping of the boats
" when the king paſſes the rivers;—and
" they

"they have the honour of bearing the
"*white silk fringe* in their arms, which,
"in France, is the *coronal colour*. The
"keys of all the cities where the king
"makes his entry are given to their cap-
"tain, in waiting, or out of waiting. He
"has the privilege, in waiting, or out of
"waiting, at ceremonies, such as corona-
"tions, marriages, and funerals of the
"kings, and at the baptisms and marriages
"of their children, to take duty upon
"him. The coronation robe belongs to
"him: and this company, by the death
"or change of a captain, never changes its
"rank, as do the three others."

It would be easy to produce the most honourable testimonies of our national character, from the writers of all the states of any note in Europe, our nearest neighbours excepted. But this much may suffice to convince the most *partial* and *credulous*

of

of Doctor Johnson's readers, that, when we began to have " trade and intercourse " with England," our manners could not stand in much need of any cultivation from that quarter. It will be allowed, I believe, that the English, like most other nations, are indebted for their *own* chief improvements to the French. It would, therefore, be ridiculous to suppose, that we, who had access to the *original* so long before themselves, should have occasion, at last, to borrow from the *copy*, and thus to acquire the little *polish* he allows us, at second-hand only.

Page 10th.—When speaking of the university of St. Andrews, the Doctor says, " That the universities in Scotland are " mouldering into dust."—This remark is the more extraordinary, as a great part of St. Salvator's college was built from the foundation not above twenty years ago.

It

It can hardly be believed, therefore, that such a visible tendency to decay could already have taken place, though, instead of solid stone, the building had been constructed of such *brittle* materials as *English* bricks.

He next complains, with more virulence than justice, of the neglected state of the *chapel* of St. Leonard's college.—But as that college has been, with great propriety, dissolved, a strict attention to its chapel, which is no longer wanted for religious purposes, does not appear necessary. The chapel of St. Salvator's, however, which, within these few years, has been very neatly repaired, and that at a confiderable expence, has entirely escaped the Doctor's notice. Not a word of this; otherwise, as it now supplies the place of the other, the dilapidation would have been accounted for, and this heinous charge of *sacrilege* shewn to be unjust. To be consistent, therefore, it was necessary to be silent. And the Doctor's tender regard to decorum, in this instance, illustrates a beautiful observation of his own, in the page I have last quoted, when he says, "Where there " is yet shame, there may in time be vir- " tue."

The *library* of St. Andrews is the next object of his remarks, which, he tells us, " is not very spacious."—This, however, is a vague and indefinite way of speaking, to which the Doctor is rather too frequently addicted. General terms convey no distinct ideas; and, if he wished to be understood, he should have given the several dimensions, that the public might judge for themselves. For my own part, I am at a loss to know what he means by *very spacious*. It is not, indeed, so spacious as *St. Paul*'s; but it is sufficiently large and elegant,

elegant, as a repofitory of books, for any literary fociety in the kingdom.

He informs us, that the gentleman by whom it was fhewn, hoped to mortify his Englifh vanity, by telling him, that they had no fuch library in England. This obfervation, I confefs, was needlefs; and, perhaps, unjuft. But, be that as it may, the Doctor feems determined to have his revenge, by faying fomething to difparage it.

Nothing can be more uncandid and erroneous, than the account he gives of the rates at which the different claffes of ftudents may pafs their feffion, or term, at St. Andrews. His calculation, in general, falls fhort of the neceffary expences, by more than one half. Formerly, perhaps, the fums he mentions might have been nearly fufficient; but it is well known, that,

that, of late years, the expence of an academical education in Scotland, as is probably the cafe in England too, has increafed very confiderably.

When a man attempts to inform the Public in any thing, he fhould take fome care to be firft well informed himfelf. But our traveller, on moft occafions, feems not to be very nice in that refpect. Minute enquiries might either be troublefome, or not fuit his purpofe; and, therefore, to cut the matter fhort, and come eafily at his point, he often makes a confident affertion ftand for authority.

The Doctor, at length, takes leave of St. Andrews; though not, to do him juftice, without making decent mention of the kindnefs of the profeffors. But even that, he fays, " did not contribute to abate " the uneafy remembrance of an univerfity " declining,

" declining, a college alienated, and a
" church profaned and haftening to the
" ground." From thefe circumftances he
is led into a train of *reveries*, which he
concludes in thefe *pathetic* words: " Had
" the univerfity been deftroyed two centu-
" ries ago, we fhould not have regretted
" it; but to fee it pining in decay and
" ftruggling for life, fills the mind with
" mournful images and ineffectual wifhes."

This is certainly fine language; and a proof, no doubt, of fine feelings. I heartily fympathize with his *generous* diftrefs, efpecially as there is no remedy but *ineffectual wifhes*. But I muft tell the *good* man, for his comfort, that the matter is not quite fo bad as his too lively imagination reprefents it; and that the *mournful images* which fill his mind, are the mere vagaries of a diftempered fancy. His readers, therefore, need not be too deeply impreffed with

with the calamities he fpeaks of; as it is not the firft time, I am told, that the Doctor has amufed the public with a *Falfe Alarm*.

But to follow our traveller a little more clofely on this fubject. What he calls *an univerfity declining*, muft certainly refer to the college of St. Leonard; for I have mentioned a little above, that the college of St. Salvator had undergone a thorough repair within thefe laft twenty years. As this, then, is what ought, in propriety, to be now called the univerfity, the other being diffolved; and as he acknowledges the the abilities of the profeffors; the moft partial, I think, muft fee the folly, as well as the falfehood of this affertion. But had thofe walls, which he defcribes as *pining in decay*, and the other univerfities in Scotland, of which he gives not a much better account, produced as few eminent men, as
fome

some other universities that might be named, the Doctor's antipathy to this country had not, perhaps, been so great; nor would he, probably, have taken the trouble of examining our seminaries of learning upon the spot.

As to his *alienated college*, he saves me the trouble of saying much on that head, by confessing (page 10.) that " the dissolution of St. Leonard's college was doubtless necessary." If this be so, why complain of the measure? To be necessary and yet a reproach, seems rather somewhat incompatible, and presents us with a combination of terms, for which, perhaps, we can find no authority, unless in the Doctor's Dictionary.

We come now, along with the Doctor, to the melancholy task of viewing " a church profaned and hastening to the ground."

ground."—This church is no other than the old chapel of the annexed, not the *alienated*, college of St. Leonard. Its having been formerly confecrated by the Romish rites, may give some little *fillip* to the Doctor's zeal; but in what manner it has been profaned of late years, unless he means by the *Presbyterian* religion, I am unable to conjecture. Since the dissolution of the seminary to which it belonged, it has ceased to be occupied as a place of worship. I see no profanation, therefore, in applying it to any other useful purpose; as no degree of sanctity can surely remain in the walls. The Scots, at least, do not carry their veneration for such *relics* so far as the Doctor did in the island of *Jona*, as we shall see in its proper place; a circumstance which is no bad index to his religious *creed*.

Page 16th. He represents " the whole country as extending in uniform nakedness, nefs, except that in the road between Kirkaldy and Cowpar, he paffed for a few yards between two hedges."—Here I could venture to lay an hundred to one, that our doughty traveller miftook two extenfive parks for two fmall hedges; from whence we may form an idea of the correctnefs of his defcription. This notable gentleman came to Scotland without eyes to fee the objects that lay in his way; and therefore to follow him through the account he gives of his journey with too much confidence, would be literally trufting to a *blind* guide.

He paffes very rapidly through the town of *Dundee*, for fear, I fuppofe, of being obliged to take notice of its increafing trade. Befides a variety of other extenfive and profitable manufactures, the dying of linen yarn is brought to a greater degree of perfection in that place, than any where else in Great Britain. As this is a very curious art, and employs some thousands of people, one would think it as deserving of notice, as many other things that attracted the Doctor's attention.

To see commerce flourish, industry rewarded, and the poor have bread, are objects which would have given pleasure to a benevolent mind; and they would have been related with rapture. But England had not yet made any great progress in this branch; and the Doctor did not choose to acknowledge, that his countrymen were in any thing outdone by the Scots. I profess, I mean nothing local in this remark. But, as the Doctor is so very ready to speak out, when the balance is on the other side; I think it but justice to claim that share of comparative merit, which his silence has here denied us.

His

His next stage was *Aberbrothick*, to which he pays a very *unusual* compliment, on account of its ancient and magnificent, but now decayed monastery; for he tells us, in page 20th, " that he should scarcely have regretted his journey, had it afforded nothing more than the sight of Aberbrothick."

I know not with what degree of pleasure the Doctor surveyed the ruins of this venerable pile; but his abrupt description of it cannot convey much to the reader, nor induce any other stranger to travel so far for the same sight. He endeavours to account for this deficiency, by pleading the approach of night, which obliged them to desist from their researches. Had there been no other day to succeed that night, this indeed might be some excuse; but it affords none for not returning next morning, to have a more complete view of an object,

object, which he owns had captivated his fancy fo much.

There was no occafion, however, to call in the affiftance of the night to conceal from his readers, a fcene which did fome credit to the country. The Doctor, while in Scotland, never faw more than he was willing to communicate. He touches very flightly, or not at all, on fuch objects as might excite the curiofity of the inquifitive; but the moft trifling handle for obloquy is greedily laid hold of, and tedioufly difplayed.

Page 21ft. At *Montrofe*, he complains much of the behaviour of the Inn-keeper. But, happily for this nation, he found out that his hoft was an Englifhman, otherwife " every mother's fon of us" would have been reprobated for his fake.

While at this place, he observes, that our beggars " solicit silently, or very modestly."—Here, one would naturally expect, he had found something to speak well of; but not so with the Doctor. He begins a harangue on the merits of the begging-trade, and concludes in favour of clamour and perseverance. When a man will not allow the silent modesty of a Scotch beggar to escape the lash, it is enough to shew that he is determined not to be pleased.

I intended to have made a remark on what I thought an impropriety in our traveller's language, when he says that " the *hedges* near Montrose are of *stone.*" But I shall leave the *thorn* of correction for the abler hand of *Lexiphanes;* a name which the Doctor may long remember, for a former *complete trimming* of his *Vocabulary*.

In his way from Montrose, he observes, "that the fields are so generally plowed, that it is hard to imagine where grass is found for the horses that till them."—Alas! what shall *poor* Scotland do to please the *good* Doctor? In one place he finds too little tillage, in another too much. Not long ago, he told us, "that the whole country was extended in uniform nakedness;" but here he seems to forget himself, and says, "the harvest, which was almost ripe appeared very plentiful." A country covered with a plentiful crop, cannot certainly be called naked. But let the reader account for such caprices, and reconcile such contradictions, if he can.

He insinuates, page 24, that there are no robbers in Scotland. But, as he seldom bestows with the one hand, without taking away with the other, he concludes his observation by adding, "But where there are

are so few travellers, why should there be robbers?"—If he means any thing by this, it must be, that the poverty with which he every where brands the Scotch nation, makes the poorer sort honest. This is one good consequence from a misfortune at least; but the conclusion will by no means follow. Riches and poverty are relative all the world over; and consequently, where there is but little wealth, the wants of the most indigent, will be as effectually relieved by depredations on their neighbours, as in more opulent countries. In spite of the Doctor's sophistry, therefore, a pretended want of inducements to rapine, fails to account here for the want of the practice. The safety with which, as he confesses, he pursued his journey, both by night and by day, called for a more *generous* interpretation. It is principle alone, and neither the penury or paucity of its inhabitants, that exempts the travel-

ler

ler in Scotland from the terrors of the piſtol and dagger.

This communicative gentleman, among other curious anecdotes, informs us, that he ſeldom found in Scotland any method of keeping their windows open, when there was occaſion for admitting freſh air, but by holding them up with the hand, unleſs now and then among good contrivers there be a nail which one might ſtick into a hole to keep them from falling.—The misfortune is, whatever the Doctor meets with but once, if it ſuits his purpoſe, he will make univerſal. That he might meet with ſome inſtances of what he mentions, I will not diſpute; nor in remote corners, nor even elſewhere when the pulhes may happen to be out of order, do I think it a bad ſhift; and if our neighbours of the South have not a *nail*, or ſome ſuch expedient, in the like circumſtances, they are not what he calls *good contrivers*.

For

For once, however, he seems to feel a conscious blush for the futility of his censures; and we find him have the *good grace* to offer an apology for abasing himself so far, as to mention such trifles as *nails* to support windows, by alleging, " that the great outlines or characteristic of a nation are to be marked out not in palaces, or among the learned, but among the bulk of the people."—This is certainly a just observation, in which I heartily agree with him; and had he begun to *mark out* these *outlines* or *characteristics* a little nearer home, he might, perhaps, have found fewer novelties on this side of the Tweed.

Page 48. He observes, " A Scotch army was very cheaply kept after the time of the Reformation."—I know not indeed, how *cheap* those armies might have been to their friends; but the history of England can vouch that they often proved very *dear* to their enemies. To be particular on this head

head would be invidious; nor shall the Doctor's malevolence provoke me to draw aside the veil which a happy union between the two kingdoms has long since, among men of sense and moderation, thrown over past transactions.

In reflecting upon the ruinous state of our cathedrals, he faces about for once, and tells the English likewise, that "their cathedrals are mouldering by unregarded dilapidation."—Here his own countrymen exclaim against his want of candour, and clearly convict him of a most audacious misrepresentation, by pointing out several large sums which have been lately expended on the reparation of some of their churches.

We have reason to complain of him in almost every page; and the present instance of his insincerity may satisfy others that we have not always had fair play. Introducing

ducing the Scots, he might hope, as the scene lies at a distance, to exercise the common, though not very honourable *privilege* of a traveller, without fear of discovery. But what shall the world think of a man who, regardless of the infamy, ventures to trespass where detection is unavoidable? A sense of shame and a regard to truth generally go together; and when a man has lost the one, he seldom retains the other.

He says, pages 50, 51, that " the first orchard and plantation of oak he saw in Scotland was at Fochabers," though it is well known there were several of both kinds in his way, had he been disposed to observe them. But where the Doctor could not get a good dinner, a circumstance which is generally thought to have an uncommon influence on his narrations, he seldom found any agreeable objects. At any rate it does not seem a very judicious situation

situation for orchards, to place them so near the road, that a person who hardly sees his finger-length before him should be able to descry them.

At *Forres*, Dr. Johnson " found nothing worthy of particular remark." Mr. *Pennant*, however, was a little more fortunate here, as well as every where else. " Near Forres," says that gentleman, " on the road side is a vast column three feet ten inches broad, and one foot three inches thick; the height above the ground is twenty-three feet; below, as is said, twelve or fifteen feet. On one side are numbers of rude figures of animals and armed men, with colours flying: some of the men seemed bound like captives. On the opposite side was a cross included in a circle, and raised a little above the surface of the same.—This is called king *Sueno*'s stone, and seems to be, as Mr. Gordon conjectures, erected by the Scots, in memory of the

the final retreat of the Danes." This monument of Scotch triumph over the Danes, who had put England under the yoke, Dr. Johnson did not see, or he did not choose to record an event so much to their honour.

Before he left Forres, he might have found something *worthy of remark* in contemplating the ruins of the old castle, which stood at the west end of the town, and was formerly a place of great extent and strength. He might likewise have entertained himself agreeably by taking a view, from the town, of the fertile plain below, which stretches for many miles towards the sea, as well as to the East and West; and where he could have seen gentlemen's seats, with *hedges, trees,* and every other mark of cultivation, scattered before him in the most delightful profusion. But the Doctor mentions none of those things, as it was not his intention to give

give his reader the least favourable idea of the grandeur of our ancestors, or the industry of the present times.

Not far from this town, in his way to Nairn, he had an opportunity of seeing the castle of *Tarnaway*, an ancient and noble seat of the Earls of Murray. Here he would have found, what he pretends so often to have looked for in vain, parks, plantations, and natural woods in abundance; which, with other beauties of nature and art, might sufficiently compensate for the trouble of a short peep as he went along; it would not have taken him much out of his way, and he would have made a shift to visit a *popish* church, or even the ruins of one, at a greater distance.

Of *Fort George*, which he owns to be the most regular in the island, he mentions little else than the good entertainment he received at the governor's table. His pretence

tence for not giving a more particular account of this important place is, " because he could not delineate it fcientifically," as he phrafes it. But the true reafon was, that he did not wifh his countrymen to know that there was any thing in the North of fo fuperior a nature, and fo well worth their feeing. Had Fort George, inftead of what it is, been the meaneft and moft irregular in the ifland, the good Doctor would have found *other* language to delineate it, if he could not be *fcientifically* exact; or, in other words, where fcience failed, farcafm would have done the reft.

Page 54.—One can hardly forbear fmiling to hear him talk of Scotland being conquered by *Cromwell*. But a man muft have little knowledge of facts, or ftill lefs honefty, who can gravely advance fuch an opinion; as it is well known to every perfon who is in the leaft acquainted with hiftory, that Scotland has never been conquered. The country has been often invaded, and its armies have been sometimes defeated, but it never yet has submitted to a foreign yoke.

To reduce Scotland was an attempt that defied the whole power of the Roman empire, even at the height of its glory. The Danes, who made so easy a conquest of England, acquired nothing but death and graves in Scotland; and the united fraud, force, and perseverance of Edward I. and some of his successors, though always assisted by a powerful faction in the country, could never subdue the spirit of a people who were determined to be free, and disdained the control of an usurper.

But in order to clear up this matter a little, it is necessary to stop the Doctor for a while, in his journey and *conquests*, and desire him, by way of prelude, to look back,

back, and see what antiquity says on the subject.

In the year 55 before Christ, when *Julius Cæsar* invaded Britain, it is known he was repulsed with considerable loss. Afterwards, in the year 165, it appears from history, that the Caledonians cut the Romans to pieces; while the English historians, however ready on most occasions to do ample justice to their country, do not pretend to say, that South Britain, at that æra, made any stand against that warlike people.

Ammianus Marcellinus owns that the North Britons killed *Follafandus*, a Roman general, and *Nectarides*, count of the maritime coast. *Theodosius*, one of the most renowned generals of the times, was then sent with a powerful army against them, and relieved the city of London, then under dreadful apprehensions from the North Britons.

After repeated attempts of the Romans to conquer the Caledonians, the emperor *Severus* went himself in person against them, in the year 208, with the strength of the whole empire; and though he had the assistance of South Britain, and of part of the south of Scotland, then Roman provinces, he was contented at last, after a loss of more than seventy thousand * men in one campaign, to treat with *them* and the Meates †, and erect a new wall to stop their incursions.

Twenty years after the death of Severus, the Caledonians were considered as such formidable enemies, that *Dio* tells us, in his account of the disposition of the Roman legions, about the year 230, that the Romans kept two legions on the borders

* *Stillingfleet*, an English writer, acknowledges on the authority of Tacitus, that the Romans lost seventy thousand men in one year, fighting against the North Britons.

† The ancient name of the people in that part of Scotland which lies on the south of the river Clyde.

against

against the unconquered Britons; whereas one legion was sufficient to keep all the rest of Britain in subjection*.

This is the account which the most candid and unexceptionable of the Roman historians give of this matter. From hence, therefore, it appears, that the Romans, even at a time when they were masters of the known world, and had attained to their highest pitch of grandeur, were sometimes obliged to compound matters with the Caledonians, and at last utterly to abandon all thoughts of conquering a people whom they generously confessed to be the most warlike they had ever encountered.

Here, I must own, I cannot help being in some pain for the poor Doctor's situation, as he must surely *strain hard* to swallow this harsh pill; and yet, disagreeable

* Lib. lv. 564.

as it is, down it muſt go, ſince this is not a ſtory founded upon *Scotch narration.*

But further, it will readily occur to the intelligent reader, that the inroads of the Romans, as well as thoſe of Edward I. hardly reached, and never went beyond *Druim-alba;* ſo that at the worſt, ſuppoſing all the tract to the ſouthward to have been completely conquered, inſtead of being only over-run ſometimes, the greateſt part of the country muſt ſtill have retained its liberty.

I am ſenſible, that with ſome a common anſwer to all this is, " that the conqueſt of Scotland was not worth while." Should Doctor Johnſon chooſe to retreat under the ſame cover, let him inform us, if he can, why ſo ſenſible a people as the Romans ſhould perſevere ſo long, and be ſo very obſtinate in their laſt effort, as to ſacrifice ſeventy thouſand men in

the

the purfuit of fo contemptible an object? And why Edward I. of England, among whofe failings folly has never been reckoned the chief, fhould have employed almoft his whole life, and wafted fo much blood and treafure, on the fame unprofitable attempt? From hence, I think, it does not feem very probable, that fuch an acquifition was formerly deemed a matter of fo little confequence; whatever may now be the opinion of a *wifer* pofterity. It muft be confeffed, however, that the *anfwer* is a *convenient* one; it is like cutting the *Gordian knot*, which could not be untied.

As to the conqueft fo ridiculoufly afcribed to *Cromwell*, little need be faid to fuch as are acquainted with the circumftances of thofe times. A powerful party of the Scots had early oppofed the impolitic meafures of the king, and they were the firft to appear in the field againft him; though from different motives, they had embarked

in

in the fame enterprife with Cromwell, and confequently there could be no ground of quarrel between them. When, therefore, that *regicide* went afterwards to the North, it was not to conquer a whole kingdom, but only to curb a party that ftill continued to act for the royal caufe; and even in that he was affifted by many of their own countrymen, who were fanguine enemies to the Houfe of *Stuart*. Had he gone with more ambitious views, and againft an united people, his expedition might have ended, like many others from the fame quarter, in a manner which Dr. Johnfon would not choofe to relate.

None furely can be weak enough to believe that Cromwell could do more in a few weeks, than the moft renowned commanders had been able to atchieve in as many centuries. The whole glory of this conqueft, therefore, muft belong to the *Doctor* alone. What could not be done in the

the field, he has accomplished in his closet, and *shamed* the sword of the soldier with one *dash* of his pen.

The Doctor next proceeds to enumerate the *many* and *great* advantages which we derived from the loss of our freedom. He says, page 55, " Cromwell civilized them by conquest, and introduced by useful violence the arts of peace:" and then, as the sum total of these *valuable arts*, he adds very gravely, " that he was told at *Aberdeen*, that the people learned from Cromwell's soldiers, to make shoes and to plant kail."

These to be sure were two very good things, as they administered at once both to our external and internal wants; but that our traveller should be told so at *Aberdeen*, seems rather a little suspicious. That has long been a city of extensive trade and frequent intercourse with the continent of Europe:

it cannot be supposed, therefore, that *the people* were strangers to the making of shoes at that period; unless we can suppose at the same time, that no such thing as shoes were then in use any where else; and that Cromwell's soldiers were afterwards dispersed among all nations, as so many *missionary coblers*, to instruct *the people* in that useful *art of peace*.

But let the Doctor's credibility stand or fall by his own testimony. He acknowledges (page 56), that the Scots are ingenious and inquisitive,—that they had early attained the liberal arts,—and excelled in ornamental knowledge. Is it consistent with such a description then, that a manual art for supplying so essential a conveniency of life, should be totally unknown to them? Even among a ruder people, the feelings of nature would certainly suggest expedients, however imperfect, to guard against the rigours of particular seasons and climates.

We come next to consider the probability of what relates to the article of *kail*. Dr. Johnson would no doubt insinuate, that kail and other garden vegetables had abounded in England long before they were cultivated in Scotland; but if he consults Anderson's History of the Rise and Progress of Commerce, he will find that our southern neighbours have so little to boast of in this particular, that in 1509 there was not a sallad in all England, and that cabbages, carrots, turnips, and other plants and roots, were imported from the Netherlands. The whole country could not furnish a single sallad, &c. for Henry the Eighth's queen, till gardeners and different sorts of plants were brought from foreign countries.

Let this be compared with what we read in a history of Scotland by John Leslie, popish bishop of Ross, who flourished in the year 1560, and dedicated his book to the pope. In the second edition of this work, printed at Rome in 1675, the Doctor will find, that in the bishop's time Glasgow was a market famous not only for wine, &c. &c. but that it likewise abounded in orchards and garden herbs *. And again, that Murray was famous for all sorts of corn, and likewise for orchards, &c †.—It is not very likely then, that a country which abounded in these things should want so ordinary an article as common kail.

From hence it appears, as bishop Leslie wrote about a century before Cromwell went to Scotland, that Dr. Johnson's account of this matter cannot be just. And indeed I am apt to think, if he had any information at all, it was a mere trick of

* Page 11. Glasguam celeberrimum emporium vini, aquæ vitæ, Brogat. &c. &c. &c. pomiferis hortis et hortensibus herbis abundans.

† Page 26. Moravia omni frumenti genere, pomiferis hortis, &c. delectat.

some

some wag, who diverted himself with his English vanity, and now laughs at his weakness for recording a Canterbury tale.

After concluding his *history* of kail, the Doctor gives a specimen of his abilities as a philosopher. "How they lived without kail," says he, "it is not easy to guess: they cultivate hardly any other plant for common tables, and when they had not kail, they probably had nothing."—What force of reasoning! how beautiful, how just the conclusion! The fable of the Chameleon needs no longer give surprise. *Air* is something to live upon; but this miracle of English erudition has found out, that a whole nation of people can live for ages upon nothing. All great discoveries, to be sure, have been reserved for that favourite spot of heaven, called England. But Dr. Johnson's *nothing* surpasses *every thing!*

In the last quoted page, he acknowledges, " that literature, soon after its revival, found its way to Scotland; and that from the middle of the sixteenth century, almost to the middle of the seventeenth, the politer studies were very diligently pursued."— The force of truth seems, for once, to have unsealed the Doctor's eye-lids. But the apparent candour of this confession is effaced by his concealing, that the Scots had likewise their share of the sciences before the subversion of learning. Such of them as were known in Europe at the time, were cultivated at I, Oronsa, and other places, so early as the fifth and sixth centuries. *Collum Cille,* or St. Columba, came to I about the year 565, and of his age the forty-third; which was an hundred and thirty-five years after the building of that abbey by *Fergus* II.

King *Edwin,* of Saxon race, first embraced Christianity only in 627; whereas it had prevailed in Scotland since 165.—*Oswald,* king of Northumberland, sent for learned men to Scotland in 634.—St. *Aidan* was

consecrated

consecrated bishop of Northumberland in 635. *Finan*, from Iona, succeeded him in 652. *Colman* succeeded Finan in 661, but retired to Scotland again in 664, when the dispute about Easter and the Tonsure was decided in the synod against him.

In the reign of *Malduinus,* who succeeded to the crown of Scotland in 668, *Buchanan* says, " the Scottish monks propagated the
" doctrines of Christ over almost all Eng-
" land, and had so instructed the English
" youth, that now they seemed able of
" themselves to preach the gospel in a
" proper manner to their countrymen;
" but their envy against their masters grew
" in proportion to their learning; and
" their prejudice in this respect went so
" far, that the Scottish monks were obliged
" to return to their own country. Though
" this contumely cut off, at that time, the
" concord between the two nations, the
" modesty of those who had received the

F 3 " insult,

" infult, kept both kingdoms from an
" open war."

From this event, the violence on one fide, and moderation on the other, the reader can eafily trace out the ancient characteriftic of the two nations; and, if we may judge from that *good temper* with which the Scots have, of late years, borne the *invectives* of their fouthern neighbours, the fame traits of national character will ftill appear uniformly to diftinguifh both. The indecent fcurrilities of a *Churchill*, a *Wilkes*, and others, and more latterly, the *coarfer* attacks of a *Johnfon*, have not hitherto met with any other mark of refentment than a filent contempt.

In the Bifhop of Rofs's book * we may fee, that about the year 273, there

* Floruere circa hæc tempora (A. D. 273) apud Scotos Amphibalus, M dacus, &c. &c. multique alii viri, doctrina et religione infignes, Dei cultores (Culdei noftra lingua vulgari dicti). Pag. 115.

flourifhed

flourished among the Scots, *Amphibalus*, *Modacus*, and many other men eminent for their learning and religion, who were worshippers of God, and called, in our common language, viz. the *Galic*, Culdich (or Culdees).

We may observe from the famous passage in Tertullian, wrote about A. D. 209, that there were already believers in Christ, even in those parts of the island which the Romans had not been able to subdue †.

Before the end of the fourth century the Christian religion was spread from one end of the province of *Valencia* to the other; a space comprehending the south-west part of Scotland, from the Solway Frith to Dunbarton. St. *Ninian* was born of Christian parents in what was afterwards called Galloway, and formed the one extremity of this province; and in the other, near Dunbarton, St. *Patrick* was also born of

† Britannorum inaccessa loca, Christo vero subdita. Tertullian. contra Judæos, cap. 7.

Chriftian parents, and in a place wholly peopled by Chriftians. And thofe two faints became, by themfelves and their difciples, the firft apoftles of the Picts and Scots, both in Scotland and in Ireland.—Laft of all, the Saxons of the north of England were alfo converted by St. Aidan, as already mentioned, in the feventh century.

Thefe few hints relative to the rife and progrefs of civilization in general, and of Chriftianity in particular, in both kingdoms, will, it is to be hoped, pull down one ftory at leaft of the Doctor's height, and fatisfy the Public that the odds, in point of time, is greatly in favour of Scotland.

Page 57.—He fays, " the Scots muft be for ever content to owe to the Englifh all their elegance and culture."—Had the Doctor been here giving an account of any other nation in Europe, I make no doubt but he would likewife have found fome opportunity of making a fimilar claim in favour

favour of *old England*. Our good neighbours have been always pretty remarkable for the *modest* virtue of self-applause, and considering their own country, at all times and in all things, as the true standard of all perfection.

What has been already said, concerning *our* early connection with France, may be a sufficient answer to the *absurdity* and *arrogance* of this assertion. It is with an ill grace, indeed, that the English pretend to be a model of taste for others: they themselves are daily copying from the *Gallic* school; and though they have been long under tutorage, the world have not yet conceived any high opinion of their *elegance and culture*. In spite of discipline, there is still a roughness in their manners which has rendered them proverbial.

But the frequent repetition of the above remark, to be found in the Doctor's performance,

formance, renders it neceffary to have recourfe to a few facts, for fetting that matter in a proper light: and, therefore, I muft recal his attention to fome circumftances relating to the ftate of the two kingdoms, long before any friendly intercourfe between them could give us an opportunity of receiving thofe *boafted* improvements.

In the year 1234, ftraw was ufed for the king's bed in England.—In 1300, wine was fold in England, only by apothecaries, as a cordial. But it was then quite otherways in Scotland, becaufe of our extenfive trade, in proportion to the commerce of thofe days, with France and Spain; and till I adverted to this circumftance, it often furprifed me to find frequent mention made, in many of our ancient *Gallic* poems, of the drinking of wine and burning of wax in the habitations of our chieftains.—In 1340, the parliamentary grants to the king of England were only in kind; and thirty thoufand thousand sacks of wool was this year's grant.—In 1505, the first shilling was coined in England.—In 1561, Queen Elizabeth wore the first pair of *knitted* silk stockings that ever were in that country.— In 1543, pins were first made in England; and before that time the ladies used *skewers*.

To all this let me oppose, but particularly to the *skewers* of the English ladies, the account which the Bishop of Ross gives of the dress of the women among the ancient Scots. We shall there find, " that " they were clothed with *purple* and *em-* " *broidery* of most exquisite workmanship, " with bracelets and necklaces on their arms " and necks, so as to make a most graceful " appearance *." Nor needs it be matter

* Mulierum habitus apud illos (scil. priscos Scotos) decentissimus erat. Nam talari tunicæ, arte phrygia ut plurimum confectæ, amplas chlamydes atque illas quidem polymitas, superinduerunt. Illarum brachia armillis, et colla monilibus elegantius ornata, maximam habent decoris speciem. Pag. 55.

" of

of surprise how the Scots had opportunities of procuring such ornaments, since the same author shews they had, at that time, a considerable trade with France and Spain, from Inverlochay, near Fort William *.

After this view of the matter, it is difficult to say, whether we are to accuse Dr. Johnson of ignorance, or insincerity, in what he has so *boldly*, but with so little appearance of justice, asserted. It is certain, had he been in the least acquainted with the history of his own country, he might easily have seen, that the English have been a little too tardy in their own improvements, to support them in any *decent* claim of having civilized their neighbours.

But notwithstanding all that can be said to the contrary, the Doctor seems deter-

***

* Ad Louchææ ostia sita olim erat opulentissima civitas Inverlothæa appellata, ad quam Galli, Hispanique, commercii causa frequentius trajecerant. Hæc postea a Norvegis, Danisque eversa, et nunquam a nobis deinceps, quæ nostra est ignavia, instauratur. Pag. 23.

mined, right or wrong, to maintain his position. He therefore goes on, and tells us again very roundly, " that till the union made the Scots acquainted with English manners, their tables were coarse as the feasts of Eskimeaux, and their houses filthy as the cottages of Hottentots."—There is an expression among lawyers, " that what proves too much, proves nothing." It is just so with my *worthy friend* the Doctor, in this place: he has laid on his *filth* so very thick, that I am of opinion it will fall off by its own weight.

But in the name of wonder, who could expect such a remark to drop from the pen of a man on whom the witty Lord *Chesterfield*, many years ago, bestowed the appellation of *Hottentot* *? His lordship was

---

* When talking of our Author, the Earl of Chesterfield said, " that he could never consider Dr. Johnson in any other point of view than as a more respectable kind of Hottentot."

allowed

allowed not only to be a good judge of character, but likewife to have a good hand at drawing a *likenefs*. It was, therefore, unlucky in our Author to come blundering out with an expreffion which muft call to our remembrance this ftriking fpecimen of the noble artift's fkill. For I will be bold to affirm, that no man has ever yet feen Dr. Johnfon in the act of *feeding*, or beheld the infide of his *cell* in *Fleet-ftreet*, but would think the *feafts of Efkimeaux* or the *cottages of Hottentots* injured by a comparifon.

But fuppofing the Doctor's charge to hold good in very diftant times, let me afk him whether England and every other country under the fun has not had its ages of *ignorance* and *barbarity?* If this *folemn* pedant will deign to look back, he will find many things in the hiftory of his own country which ought to convince him that civilization did not begin very

very early there, nor advance with a quick pace. I am always forry when I am obliged to trace out anecdotes of this kind; but his ill-manners and want of candour render it neceffary.

Alfred the Great, who died in the year 900, complained " that from the Humber to the Thames there was not a prieft that underftood the Liturgy in his mother-tongue; and that from the Thames to the fea there was not one that could tranflate the eafieft piece of Latin. This univerfal ignorance, and the little relifh the Englifh had for arts and fciences, made the King invite learned and ingenious foreigners."— In 1167 King Henry the Second fends to Ireland, and caufes build a palace of *wattles* in Dublin, after the manner of the country, wherein he keeps his Chriftmas.—It was not till 1209 that London began to be governed by a Mayor;—and fo near our own

own times as the year 1246 moſt of the houſes in that capital were thatched with *ſtraw*,—the windows were without glaſs,—and all the fires ſtood to the wall without *chimneys*.—In the year 1300, and afterwards, almoſt all the houſes in England were built of wood, &c. &c.

Such facts as theſe are the fureſt teſts of the progreſs of civilization in any country, as they ſhew the taſte and manners of the inhabitants at different periods of time. If the Doctor doubts their authenticity, he will find them confirmed by *Rapin* and other hiſtorians.

As our traveller gives us only his own authority for what he ſays of Scotland at the time of the union, a teſtimony which the reader, by this time, cannot think altogether unexceptionable; let us now ſee what others have reported of the ſtate of civilization

civilization among us long before that period.

When *Margaret*, daughter of *Henry* the Seventh of England, became the Queen of our *James* the Fourth, she was attended to the Scotch court by many of the first nobility of both sexes; and yet the English historians of those days allow, that they were fully equalled, or even excelled, by the Scotch nobility, in politeness of manners, the number of their jewels, and the richness of their dress; and particularly, that the entertainments they received at the houses of our great people did not yield to any thing they had ever seen.

In 1546, *Contarini* was Pope's legate in Scotland; and upon his return to the continent, he celebrated the Scotch nation as a *polite* and *hospitable* people. He bore this testimony to their merit, though he could not succeed in the object of his embassy;

bassy; which was, to support the Romish religion, then fast declining in that kingdom, on account of the intolerable cruelties of Cardinal Betoun. But this prelate, very unlike to Dr. *Johnson*, could not permit his prejudices as an ambassador to warp his veracity as a man.

The Queen of *James* the Fifth, though a princess of so civilized a nation as France, acknowledged, " that the court and inhabitants of Scotland were the most *polite* and *civilized* she had ever seen, and the palace of Linlithgow the most *magnificent*."

As a further specimen of our *tables*, let us take the Earl of Athole's feast to James the Fifth, as related by Lindsay the historian.

The Earl of Athole's Feast to James V.

" Syne (then) the next summer the
" King past to the Highland to hunt in
" Athole,

" Athole, and took with him his mother,
" Margaret Queen of Scotland, and an
" Embaſſador of the Pope's, who was in
" Scotland for the time. The Earl of
" Athole, hearing of the King's coming,
" made great proviſion in all things per-
" taining to a Prince, that he was as well
" ſerved and eaſed, with all things neceſ-
" ſary to his eſtate, as he had been in his
" own palace of Edinburgh. For I heard
" ſay, this noble Earl gart (cauſed) make
" a curious palace to the King, to his
" mother, and to the Embaſſador, where
" they were ſo honourably eaſed and lodged
" as they had been in England, France,
" Italy, or Spain, concerning the time,
" and equivalent for their hunting and
" paſtime; which was builded in the midſt
" of a fair meadow, a fair palace of green
" timber, wind with green birks, that
" were green both under and above; which
" was faſhioned in four quarters, and in
" every quarter and nuik thereof a great
" round,

" round, as it had been a block-house,
" which was lofted and gefted the fpace of
" three houfe height; the floors laid with
" green fcarets and fpreats, medwarts
" and flowers, that no man knew whereon
" he zeid, but as he had been in a garden.
" Further, there were two great rounds in
" ilk fide of the gate, and a great port-
" culleis of tree, falling down with the
" manner of a barrace, with a draw-bridge,
" and a great flank of water of fixteen
" foot deep, and thirty foot of breadth.
" And alfo this palace within was hung
" with fine tapeftry and arraffes of filk,
" and lighted with fine glafs windows in
" all airths (directions); that this palace was
" as pleafantly decored with all neceffaries
" pertaining to a Prince, as it had been
" his own palace-royal at home. Further,
" this Earl gart make fuch provifion for
" the King, and his mother, and the Em-
" baffador, that they had all manner of
                                    " meats,

" meats, drinks and delicates that were to
" be gotten at that time, in all Scotland,
" either in burgh or land; that is to say,
" all kind of drink, as ale, beer, wine both
" white and claret, malvery, muskadel,
" hippocras and aqua vitæ. Further, there
" was of meats, white-bread, main-bread,
" and ginge-bread, with fleshes, beef,
" mutton, lamb, veal, venison, goose,
" grice, capon, coney, cran, swan, par-
" tridge, plover, duck, drake, brisse-cock,
" and pawnies, black-cock and muir-fool
" cappercaillies: and also the stanks that
" were round about the palace were full
" of all delicate fishes, as salmonds, trouts,
" pearches, pikes, eels, and all other kind
" of delicate fishes that could be gotten in
" fresh waters; and all ready for the ban-
" ket. Syne were there proper stewards,
" cunning baxters, excellent cooks and
" potengars, with confections and drugs
" for their deferts: and the halls and
" chambers

" chambers were prepared with costly bed-
" ding, vessel and napery, according for a
" king; so that he wanted none of his
" orders more than he had been at home
" in his own palace. The King remained
" in this wilderness, at the hunting, the
" space of three days and three nights,
" and his company, as I have shewn. I
" heard men say, it cost the Earl of
" Athole, every day, in expences a thou-
" sand pounds.

" The Embassador of the Pope, seeing
" this great banquet and triumph which
" was made in the wilderness, where there
" was no town near by twenty miles,
" thought it a great marvel, that such a
" thing should be in Scotland, considering
" that it was named the end of the world
" by other countries; and that there should
" be such honesty and policy in it, especially
" in the Highland, where there was so much
" wood and wilderness. But most of all,
" this

" this Embaſſador marvelled to ſee, when
" the King departed, and all his men took
" their leave, the Highland-men ſet all
" this fair place on a fire, that the King
" and the Embaſſador might ſee it. Then
" the Embaſſador ſaid to the King, " I
" marvel, Sir, that you ſhould thole (ſuffer)
" yon fair place to be burnt, that your Grace
" has been ſo well lodged in." Then the
" King anſwered the Embaſſador, and ſaid,
" It is the uſe of our Highland-men,
" though they be never ſo well lodged,
" to burn their lodging when they de-
" part." See Lindſay's Hiſtory of Scot.
p. 266, &c.

From theſe circumſtances it may appear, ſhould the Journey to the *Hebrides* ſurvive its author, how miſerably deceived they muſt be, who, in future times, ſhall take the Doctor's account of Scotland for truth. When, therefore, he boaſts of the advantages which, in theſe reſpects, the

Scots have derived from the union, he ought to have assigned a cause, why we were less refined in the beginning of the eighteenth century, than our forefathers have been proved to have been some centuries before. Either, then, he is unacquainted with our *ancient* manners, or he grossly misrepresents our *modern* character. His ignorance, therefore, or his malice, whichever the Doctor shall think the most eligible, can only account for the presumption of his assertions.

But were we to admit, with our traveller, that the English have taught us how to procure any of the *good things* of this life, it might fairly be said, that they have likewise taught us the art of *spending* them. We daily see more of a clumsy affectation, tasteless extravagance, and giddy dissipation, which many of our countrymen carry home with them from the south side of the Tweed, than of polite improvements, or useful

useful inventions. If these are the advantages which Dr. Johnson means to charge against us in favour of the English, as the *precious* effects of the union, he has an undoubted right to persist in his claim, and we are ready to acknowledge ourselves their debtors.

At the same time, we do not mean to disclaim all advantages from the union, but only to shew, that they are not of that kind which Dr. Johnson insinuates. Considered in a political light, it was certainly a wise and salutary measure for both kingdoms; but, even in that view, the English are the principal gainers. The Doctor cannot well deny this position, if he but recollects, that the English were the first to propose the union, and that it was at length carried with difficulty in Scotland. They call themselves a *generous* people; but we cannot suppose them to be so very extravagantly so, as to take so much pains
in

in pressing a measure, from which WE were to reap the chief advantages. If this really was the case, they had surely a much greater *love* and *affection* for their fellow-subjects of the North in the reign of Queen *Anne*, than, I am afraid, they possess for them in the reign of *George* the Third— if we are to judge of the whole nation from the sample given us by Dr. *Johnson*, who is reckoned one of their wisest and best men.

Page 58 brings our traveller to a road upon which " no wheel had ever rolled." There can appear nothing extraordinary in this remark, unless the good Doctor had asserted, at the same time, that every bye-road in England was fit for a carriage. We have already seen, that in 1300 all the houses in England were built of wood; and long after that period it was accounted a sort of luxury to ride in a two-wheeled cart. Besides, if we may credit even

English

English historians, their favourite Queen Elizabeth had no other mode of travelling, than by riding behind one of her domestics; which evidently shews, that the *rolling of wheels* has not been so very long known, or generally practised, even in England itself. But further, I am credibly informed, that within these forty years, a time, I presume, within the Doctor's remembrance, most of the roads within twenty miles of London were hardly fit for riding, much less for carriages. Who then but our traveller could remark, that, in the remote and unfrequented parts of the mountains of Scotland, there were not regular post roads?

In page 60 he finds out, that " civility seems part of the national character of Highlanders." If ever Dr. *Johnson* has his good-humoured intervals, this compliment certainly escaped him in one of them. But how are we to reconcile this with

with the epithets of rude, barbarous, grofs, and favage, &c. which, in other parts of his work, he fo liberally beftows on the whole nation? If the decent behaviour of common *horfe-hirers*, to ufe a Scottifh expreflion, who attended him in his journey, extorted this confeffion from him, we cannot well fuppofe, that he found the better fort of people deficient in agreeable qualifications. Either, then, the Doctor means fomething by the *civility* of his horfe-hirers, which is not underftood by others, or his national epithets can have no foundation in truth. We fhould, therefore, be glad to hear him give fome confiftent explanation of thefe particulars; as the *civility* of a *rude* and *barbarous*, or, in other words, of an *uncivilized* people, conveys an uncommon fort of idea. For my part, I have looked into his own Dictionary, and could not find, even in that *perverter* of the Englifh language, any definition of the above

above terms that can make them hang together.

When riding along the side of *Loch Nefs*, a ray of good-humour seems to have stolen into the Doctor's mind. For a while we find him pleased with the goodness of the road, and the cheerfulness of the day; but this sudden gleam, like sunshine before a storm, was of short duration. His natural gloominess soon returns; and his restless caprice finds a thousand faults. At that season of the year no mortal, but himself, could have quarrelled with the objects around him. If ever the wild magnificence of nature could please, that day's journey furnished ample matter of entertainment. Even his own description of the scene through which he passed, in spite of all his endeavours to the contrary, conveys enough to the mind of the reader to make him regret that he has not a more perfect view.

He

He gives, here and there, a peep of some beauties which he saw; but unluckily, as on most other occasions, he seems less willing to exhibit these at full length, than to point out a " rock sometimes towering in horrid nakedness."

From the banks of *Loch Ness* the Doctor turns his observation to its waters. He had been told at Fort Augustus, that it continues open in the hardest winters, though another lake not far from it is covered with ice. This being an exception from the common course of things, he seems much disposed to doubt the fact; for he will not suffer nature to sport with her own laws in Scotland, except in producing deformities. Then, indeed, she may play as many wild pranks as she thinks proper; and she pleases him the better, the more, like himself, she becomes a *Rambler*.

As there could be no motive to deceive him in a matter of so little consequence to the country, as the freezing or *not* freezing of *Loch Ness*, it is strange he should expose his own weakness, by taking so much pains to render it doubtful. He disputes this trivial fact with a solemnity truly ridiculous. At length, however, finding himself unable to give any *decent* colour to his objections, he endeavours to account for so singular a *phenomenon*; though still with this cautious *proviso*, " if it be true." But this he does in a manner so very unphilosophical, as clearly shews, either that natural inquiries have not made a great part of the Doctor's studies, or that his genius is not much adapted to such nice researches. Every man has his peculiar gift from nature; and to compile vocabularies of compound *hard* words, seems to be the task which she has allotted for our traveller. He ought therefore to confine
himself

himself to his proper province, remembering the maxim,—*ne sutor ultra crepidam.*

In Glenmorison, the Doctor seems surprised, that the innkeeper's daughter shewed no sort of embarrassment in his presence. So, indeed, are most others who have read that passage, as she certainly had never seen " *his like*" before. But the little *gipsy*, it seems, was not to be moved by the *elegance* of his figure, the *softness* of his address, or the *splendour* of his reputation. She was saucy enough to appear perfect mistress of herself, without betraying the least mark of diffidence, confusion, or the *melting* power of love.

At this place he takes care to refresh our memory with his bounty to the soldiers, whom he passed on the road, and who came to the same inn to spend the evening. One would be tempted to think, that acts of generosity are but rare things with the Doctor,

Doctor, when he dwells so ostentatiously on this trifling piece of liberality.

In page 58, he discovers what seems to have been one of his motives for undertaking his journey, namely, an inclination to dissuade all such strangers as would be directed by him from ever visiting Scotland, as being altogether unworthy of the attention of the curious. In proof of this he says, " that uniformity of barrenness can afford little amusement to the traveller; that it is easy to sit at home and conceive rocks, and heath, and waterfalls; and that these journeys are useless labours, which neither impregnate the imagination nor enlarge the understanding."

If rocks, heath, and waterfalls constitute uniformity, I should be glad to learn from the Doctor wherein variety consists? As to his reasoning in the above passage, he saves me the trouble of a refutation, by having immediately after refuted himself. After the easy mode of information which he had proposed, viz. by sitting at home and conceiving what we pleased, who would expect to hear him, in the same page, express himself as follows? " But these ideas are always incomplete, and, till we have compared them with realities, we do not know them to be just. As we see more, we become possessed of more certainties, and consequently gain more principles of reasoning, and found a wider basis of analogy. Regions mountainous and wild, thinly inhabited, and little cultivated, make a great part of the earth; and he that has never seen them, must live unacquainted with much of the face of nature, and with one of the great scenes of human existence." Let the reader now judge of the consistency between this language and what he had before asserted,—" that these journies are useless labours, which neither impregnate the imagination nor enlarge the underſtanding."

We have oftener than once ſeen the Doctor in the ſame aukward ſituation, ſaying and unſaying in the ſame breath. Who but himſelf would not have drawn his pen through the former lines, after adding the latter? But he ſeems to be above cancelling any thing he has once ſet down; otherwiſe he is too indolent to give himſelf the trouble of correction.

After endeavouring to impreſs the mind of his reader with the wildneſs of the hills of Glenmoriſon, he ſeems afraid of having ſaid too much, and making the country appear too remarkable, even by allowing it to be ſo very mountainous. He therefore inſtantly ſweeps away this negative compliment by aſking,—" yet what are theſe hillocks to the ridges of Taurus, or theſe ſpots of wildneſs to the deſarts of America?"

America?" This churlish author will not allow us to excel even in wildness.

It was in these hills, while sitting on a bank to let the horses rest, about the middle of the day, that the Doctor tells us he "first conceived the thought of his narration." Should we pay his veracity the compliment of believing this to be true, we must certainly allow him to be endowed with a retentive memory. There are so many *minutiæ* in the preceding part of *his narration*, that it is surprising they could occur without the assistance of some previous *memorandums*; and yet we can see no reason for his being at that trouble, before he had conceived the thought of making use of them.

Speaking still of the same spot, he says, " We were in this place at ease and by choice, and had no evils to suffer or to fear." If this was really so, how can he

say

say afterwards, page 98, that the Highlanders live by theft and robbery? It was certainly very bold in the Doctor to fear nothing, in the midst of their wildest mountains, if the character he gives the inhabitants be just. But, indeed, it is not easy for any reader, who is unacquainted with the country, to form any consistent idea of the people from Dr. *Johnson*'s vague and contradictory accounts of them.

Pages 98, 99, he says, that "thirty years ago no herd had ever been conducted through the mountains, without paying tribute in the night to some of the clans." This, however, is a gross misrepresentation. There are many people still living, who drove hundreds of cattle through the mountains long before that period, and never once paid the tribute he mentions. Here, therefore, we may retort upon himself the substance of a *sage* observation, which, in page 63, he applies to the Highlanders

landers concerning the freezing of *Loch Nefs*; and that is, that accuracy of narration is not very common with him, and that he is seldom so rigidly philosophical as not to represent as constant, what is sometimes only casual.

He acknowledges, page 100, that "the different clans were unconnected with the general syftem, and accustomed to reverence only their own lords." If this really was so, their quarrels with their neighbours, and the mutual injuries resulting from them, are to be explained on the same liberal principles as those which daily happen between the most independent states. The rule of morality is the same in both cases; and injury always justifies retaliation, whether we speak of the Highland clans, or of larger communities.

Under the same head, in speaking of the power of the chiefs, he says, "those who

had

had thus the difpenfation of law, were by confequence themfelves lawlefs. Their vaffals had no fhelter from outrages or oppreffions; but were condemned to endure, without refiftance, the caprice of wantonnefs, and the rage of cruelty." Here the Doctor betrays his total ignorance of the ancient law of chieftainry. The chiefs, or difpenfers of laws, as he calls them, knew their own intereft much better than ever to think of adopting the Doctor's tyrannical plan. They were under a neceffity of acting in a much more humane and mild manner towards their clans, or people, as they knew that their own fecurity and importance depended on their attachment; and that, without that, their power and influence would be nothing. Even he himfelf confeffes, page 195, " that the laird was the father of his clan." I leave it to himfelf to reconcile fo glaring a contradiction; and to convince the world,

world, if he can, that a cruel *oppreſſor* and a kind *father* are one and the ſame thing.

In page 109 he mentions an old anecdote, which, he ſays, he was told at Sir Alexander Macdonald's table, and which relates to a very barbarous effect of the feuds between two of the clans, if in reality ſuch an event ever exiſted; though, at the ſame time, we are not to ſuppoſe that the ſame ſpirit of revenge, in thoſe remote and leſs poliſhed times, was peculiar to the Highlands. But be that as it may, he takes occaſion to make the following remark: " Narrations like this," ſays he, " however uncertain, deſerve the notice of a traveller, becauſe they are the only records of a nation that has no hiſtorians, and afford the moſt genuine repreſentation of the life and character of the ancient Highlanders."

Here

Here it is obfervable, that the Doctor admits the teftimony of Highlanders, becaufe, in his opinion, it makes againft their country. But had the matter been in their favour, he would neither have recorded nor believed it.

It may, perhaps, be true, that Highlanders in general have been too negligent in committing to writing what related to their country. In remote ages, they trufted too much to their *Bards* and *Seannachies*, as other nations then did. What they wrote at *Iona* and elfewhere, on that and other fubjects, was deftroyed by various accidents. Hiftorians affirm, that *Iona* fuffered fix different devaftations in the tenth century alone. What efcaped thofe ravages was carried away either by that *generous* friend to learning and the Scots nation, Edward the Firft, in the fame fpirit of meeknefs in which he butchered the *Welch Bards*, or afterwards by Oliver Cromwell,

Cromwell, and other scourges and destroyers of antiquities, who wanted to abolish every monument of the ancient independence of this nation; or, lastly, by our own priests at the time of the Reformation.

Every thing relating to the Highlands, in particular, has met with many discouragements of late years. This, no doubt, has occasioned many other valuable vouchers to be buried in an oblivion, from which, in all probability, we shall never be able to recover them.

The Doctor is egregiously mistaken when he says that the Highlanders have no particular historians. It seems he has never heard of *Macaulay*, the two *Macphersons*, *Martin*, the *Dean* of the Isles, &c. It is to the historical and other *superior* merits of some of these gentlemen, that their country is indebted for so much of the Doctor's *critical* regard. Had they never

never written so well, he had never been so scurrilous. *Hinc illæ lachrymæ! Buchannan* too was a Highlander; as was likewise *St. Ninian*, who was born in Galloway, then an Highland country; and *St. Patrick* was born near Dunbarton.

His observations in the four following pages are of so extraordinary a nature, and furnish such unequivocal proofs of his rancour and malevolence, that I shall give them at full length.

Pages 110, 111, 112, 113.—" My inquiries about brogues gave me an early specimen of Highland information. One day I was told, that to make brogues was a domestic art, which every man practised for himself, and that a pair of brogues was the work of an hour. I supposed that the husband made brogues as the wife made an apron, till next day it was told me, that a brogue-maker was a trade, and that

a pair

a pair would coſt half a crown. It will eaſily occur, that theſe repreſentations may both be true, and that in ſome places men may buy them, and in others make them for themſelves; but I had both the accounts in the ſame houſe within two days.

"Many of my ſubſequent inquiries upon more intereſting topics ended in the like uncertainty. He that travels in the Highlands may eaſily ſaturate his ſoul with intelligence, if he will acquieſce in the firſt account. The Highlander gives to every queſtion an anſwer ſo prompt and peremptory, that ſcepticiſm itſelf is dared into ſilence, and the mind ſinks before the bold reporter in unreſiſting credulity; but if a ſecond queſtion is ventured, it breaks the enchantment; for it is immediately diſcovered, that what was told ſo confidently was told at hazard, and that ſuch fearleſſneſs of aſſertion was either the ſport of of negligence, or the refuge of ignorance.

"If individuals are thus at variance with themselves, it can be no wonder that the accounts of different men are contradictory. The traditions of an ignorant and savage people have been for ages negligently heard, and unskilfully related. Distant events must have been mingled together, and the actions of one man given to another. These, however, are deficiencies in story, for which no man is now to be censured. It were enough, if what there is yet opportunity of examining were accurately inspected, and justly represented; but such is the laxity of Highland conversation, that the enquirer is kept in continual suspense, and, by a kind of intellectual retrogradation, knows less as he hears more."

In this *learned* harangue on the *important* subject of *brogue-making*, the Doctor makes
a *double*

a *double discovery*. First, he shews, that two different accounts may be given of the same thing, and yet both may be true. In the next place, he proves, after making this acknowledgment, that the subsequent part of his criticism has no object; and, consequently, that it is as nugatory in itself as his conclusions are false and improbable. To make a silly story about the art of brogue-making the test of national candour and sincerity, is too ridiculous for any pen but that of Dr. *Johnson*.

It is true, in order to account, in some measure, for his going *beyond his last*, he tells us, that many of his subsequent inquiries upon more interesting topics ended in the like uncertainty. It were well if he had mentioned what these interesting topics were, to whom his inquiries were addressed, and what answers he received. A knowledge of these circumstances would enable us to decide more certainly on the merits of of his succeeding remarks. The Doctor, less anxious, perhaps, to " saturate his soul with intelligence," than to satiate his prejudices against Scotland with the means of misrepresentation, might have adopted such a mode of inquiry as would best answer his purpose.

He might, for instance, question one of his *brogue-makers* concerning some nice point of antiquity, to which the poor fellow could make but a very imperfect answer. The next *taylor* he met with might vary, in some circumstances, from the former; and a third person, not better informed than either of them, might differ a little from both. What then? Is there any thing surprising or uncommon in all this? Or can such a variation in the accounts of illiterate mechanics justify the Doctor's general inference, " that there can be no reliance upon Highland narration?"

Should

Should there remain the least doubt upon this head, let me suppose, for argument's sake, that I am making a similar tour through some parts of England. In the course of my travels, I see the ruins of some old abby, or, as the Doctor would more *elegantly* express it, the " dilapidated remains of ancient sanctity." I wish to know something of its history, and accost the first labourer I find in the neighbouring fields to obtain information: he gives me very honestly, no doubt, some confused *scraps* of what he had heard concerning it; but his story is full of perplexity, and several parts of it differ considerably from others. I then inquire of one after another, but with little better success. At length, tired with the deficiencies and contradictions of former accounts, I apply to the 'Squire and Parson of the parish; hoping, from men of their more enlarged notions, to have my curiosity fully satisfied. Their tales are more plausible, plaufible, but ftill defective, and differ, in feveral particulars, from each other. I find myfelf, therefore, obliged to fit down in the dark, and go in fearch of other objects of curiofity fomewhere elfe. But, wherever I go, I often meet with the fame difappointments.

That this might fometimes be the fate of a traveller in England, or, indeed, in any other country, none, I believe, will pretend to doubt. Were I, therefore, inclined to revenge my fruftrated inquiries, by making ufe of the Doctor's *illiberal* pencil, it would be eafy to delineate the Englifh character in the fame unfavourable colours. I am fure, in doing fo, I fhould do the people of that country much injuftice; but I fhould have exactly the fame reafons for charging them, in the lump, with ignorance and a difregard to truth. Becaufe every man I met with could not anfwer every queftion I chofe to put to him,

him, I might pronounce them all a nation of blockheads. And becaufe different men differed a little fometimes in their *relations* of facts, I might fay, with the fame peremptory affurance as hath been faid by our Author above, that " fuch is the laxity of Englifh converfation, that the inquirer is kept in continual fufpenfe, and, by a kind of intellectual retrogradation, knows lefs as he hears more."

Befides, it deferves to be confidered, that many of thofe whom the Doctor thought proper to interrogate, might not have Englifh enough to underftand his queftions, or return diftinct anfwers; that others might not be competent judges of the fubjects propofed to them, and confequently might give defective or erroneous accounts, from a too forward zeal to oblige a ftranger as far as they were able; and, likewife, that, even among the higher and more intelligent ranks of people, it was

weak

weak and abfurd to expect an uniformity of narration. Men, according to their opportunities, derive their knowledge from different fources. Authors themfelves are not always agreed in their communications upon the fame topics. We cannot therefore fuppofe that their readers will think alike.

A judicious author would have attended to thefe things, to avoid the imputation of malice or folly to himfelf. When a man attempts to traduce a whole people, he ought to ftand upon firm ground. But here, amidft a number of bold affertions, there is not a fingle fact produced, which will not apply to any fpot on the face of the earth, as well as to the Highlands of Scotland. By endeavouring to prove too much, therefore, the Doctor proves nothing; as fuch indifcriminate abufe can never obtain credit, even with the moft credulous. The excefs of his rancour has effectually

effectually defeated its own purpose; and he is literally in the situation of those reptiles, which, as naturalists tell us, are sometimes poisoned by their own stings.

As the Doctor acknowledges he was every where hospitably received by the Highlanders, let the world judge of the man, by this sample of his gratitude for their civilities. To search for information among the lower orders of the people, to tamper with their simplicity, to lie in wait for their answers, and catch at every trifling incoherence in their discourse, was, beyond description, mean and ungenerous. But to do all this with the insidious purpose of retailing *their* crude opinions to the public, as the standard of all Highland learning and science, is a species of literary assassination, with which the world was not acquainted before the Doctor published his Journey.

There

There is one excuse, however, for this part of our Author's conduct, and that is, that it was unavoidable. He had one favourite purpose to serve, of which I shall take notice in its proper place; and to pave the way for that, it was necessary to discredit all Highland narration. When the Doctor has an object in view, nothing must stand in his way; he goes on with giant strides. Probability, truth, and decorum must yield to his stubborn resolution, and all be sacrificed to his insolence, caprice, or disgust. When his prejudices operate, we look in vain for those restraints, either from shame or virtue, which regulate the writings of others. He can be absurd without a blush, and unjust without remorse.

Before I dismiss this article, I will just take notice of, what one would least expect, an inaccuracy in the Doctor's language. In the passage last quoted, he says he was told,

told, "that a brogue-maker was a trade." He certainly meant to have said, that *brogue-making* was a *trade*. This, however, is but a trifling flip of his pen, and the mere effect of inadvertency; nor do I mention it with any design to make it an object of criticism. I wish the same *innocent* carelessness could be pleaded for more material mistakes.

Page 113, in speaking of the *garb act*, he says, "The same poverty that made it then difficult for them to change their clothing, hinders them now from changing it again." The truth is, however, that an attachment to their ancient garb made the first change disagreeable, and not willingly complied with; and a second change, at the time alluded to, was still prevented by a British act of parliament, which the Doctor seems willing to overlook, that he might have an opportunity, according to his usual candour, of

assigning

assigning a more *favourable* reason of his own.

Page 116, he says, "The summer can do little more than feed itself, and winter comes with its cold and its scarcity upon families very slenderly provided." As the Doctor never spent a winter in the *Hebrides*, it is somewhat extraordinary, how he should pretend to know so much of the distresses of that season. But those who have passed what he calls *the dark months* in those parts, could tell a very different tale. A particular provision must be made for the winter every where; and that, together with what the summer can spare, and which greatly exceeds what the Doctor would insinuate, makes the short days, in the *Hebrides*, as comfortable as any part of the year.

In the same page he proceeds to observe, " It is incredible how soon the account of any event is propagated in these narrow countries by the love of talk, which much leisure produces, and the relief given to the mind, in the penury of insular conversation, by a new topic. The arrival of strangers at a place so rarely visited, excites rumour, and quickens curiosity. I know not whether we touched at any corner where fame had not already prepared us a reception." Here it is to be observed, that the hospitality and civility, which have been universally allowed to predominate among Highlanders, since the first accounts we have had of them, are excluded from any share in their desire of seeing strangers. He says, curiosity was their chief motive. This may pass well enough with the superficial; but with more observant readers it will not do, as he unluckily tells us, in page 238, that the same people are *totally void of curiosity*.

Page 120, he says, "There are no houses in the islands where travellers are entertained for money." This, I suppose, he would reckon no great disappointment. He had occasion to expend but very little money in Scotland; and that *little* he always mentions with regret. But did he inquire for inns at Broad-ford, Port-ree, or Dunvegan? I apprehend not. He knew he might have found them there; and so he did not chuse to hazard the question, as he wished to have an apology for living in a more *private* and less *expensive* manner. With his usual inconsistency, however, he acknowledges, in page 151, that he dined at a public-house.

Page 128, he tells us, that "the military ardour of the Highlanders is extinguished." I should be glad to know upon what the Doctor founds this assertion. The contrary is so universally acknowledged, that few of his own countrymen, I believe,

I believe, will allow it to be juſt. The laſt war bears ample teſtimony to their valour, and proves that they ſtill retain the ſpirit of their anceſtors. The ſucceſſes of that glorious period have been aſcribed, in a great meaſure, to their bravery. Prince *Ferdinand* has diſtinguiſhed them by public thanks in the field. Every other General under whom they ſerved has been laviſh in *encomiums* on their courage, and the uncommon intrepidity of their behaviour. The *Britiſh* ſenate itſelf has recorded their praiſes. And in particular the panegyric of Mr. *Pitt*, ſpoken in the Houſe of Commons a little before he was created Earl of *Chatham*, is a monument to their military fame, which defies the impudent but feeble attacks of a *pedant*'s envy and malice.

In the ſame page he ſays, " Of what the Highlanders had before the late conqueſt of their country, there remain only their language and their poverty." What he here dignifies

dignifies with the name of conquest, is the defeat of a few rebels at Culloden. Because an handful of malcontents, who had taken up arms, were routed and dispersed, is the Doctor hardy enough to call *that* a national conquest? The general loyalty of the Scotch, at that time, rendered a general conquest as unnecessary as a general resistance would have rendered it impracticable. But this is much of a piece with his *Cromwellian* conquest, which has been already disproved. It is truly pitiable to find a man of his years, and reputed erudition, so blinded by prejudice, as gravely to advance for facts what the most illiterate cannot believe, and every school-boy could confute.

He takes every opportunity to inculcate the poverty of the Scotch. This seems to be a *rich* topic to him; and, without it, I know not how he could have eked out his work. It is so often obtruded upon the reader,

reader, and that too when he would least expect it, that one must naturally think there was a want of other matter. When, therefore, he labours most to prove *their* poverty as a people, he infallibly proves his *own* as an author, at the same time.

He introduces this subject very unnecessarily, as usual, in the last quotation. I shall just contrast what he says there with some other passages from himself, and leave the reader to draw his own inference. At the bottom of page 121, and the beginning of page 122, he says, " He that shall complain of his fare in the *Hebrides*, has improved his delicacy more than his manhood."—In page 124, " The breakfast is a meal in which the Scots, whether of the Lowlands or mountains, must be confessed to excel us. The tea and coffee are accompanied not only with butter, but with honey, conserves, and marmalades. If an epicure could remove by a wish, in quest

quest of sensual gratifications, wherever he had supped he would breakfast in Scotland."—Page 125, " A dinner in the Western Islands differs very little from a dinner in England."

Here we have the most undoubted proofs not only of plenty, but of elegance. What now is become of that *poverty* into which the Doctor had so *unmercifully* plunged us but a little ago? His charity has at length prevailed; and the same hand that had sunk us so low, has raised us at once to affluence. When a man is so much at variance with himself, the least we can say is, that his testimony can have but little effect. But, as I have promised, I will not take up time in pointing out inconsistencies, which cannot escape the most careless observer.

Page 129, he says, " A longer journey than to the Highlands must be taken by him whose curiosity pants for savage virtues and barbarous grandeur." As the Doctor, in many places before, had so liberally bestowed the epithets *rude, savage,* and *barbarous* upon the Highlanders, one would think, from the softening strain of this passage, that our traveller, after a more intimate acquaintance with them, had found reason to alter his style, and consequently that there would be a truce with *scurrilities* for the future. But many of the following pages will shew, that there is no such reformation in the Doctor's language. This is but a short suspension, not an entire cessation, of obloquy and abuse. He only elevates a little, to make the fall the greater; and *his* compliments, like the tears of the *crocodile,* are but a deceitful prelude to an approaching sacrifice.

Page 151, our traveller comes to *Dunvegan,* where, he says, he was agreeably entertained by Lady *Macleod,* " who had resided

resided many years in England, and knew all the arts of southern elegance, and all the modes of English œconomy." This manner of accounting for the goodness of his reception is, at best, but a bad compliment to that lady, as *Old England* is made to run away with more than half the praise.

But there is something as nationally *invidious* in the above remark, as it is indelicate to Lady *Macleod*. It certainly is intended to insinuate, that he had found the bulk of our *Scotch-bred* ladies deficient in point of accomplishments. If he did not mean thus much, I should be glad to know what he meant by so improper an introduction of a *long residence in England*, to set off Lady *Macleod*'s character. Had he already forgot the ladies of *Raasay*, whom he had left but a day or two before, and whom he often mentions in a manner that seems to render a *residence in England* nowise

nowise necessary for attaining all the arts of elegance, and the modes of a perfect œconomy? But his own words will make the best comment upon this subject. In finishing his description of *Raasay*, he says, page 149, " Such a seat of hospitality, amidst the winds and waters, fills the imagination with a delightful contrariety of images. Without is the rough ocean and the rocky land, the beating billows and the howling storm; within is plenty and elegance, beauty and gaiety, the song and the dance."

Page 154, " A Highland laird," he says, " made a trial of his wife for a certain time, and if she did not please him, he was then at liberty to send her away." As there never was a law in Scotland authorising such a custom, the Doctor should have told us where he had made this wonderful discovery. He gives one instance, indeed, of a gentleman sending back

back his wife to her friends; and most other countries, I believe, could furnish many; but the bad consequences of the feud occasioned, on this account, between the two different clans, even as related by himself, is sufficient to prove, that the practice could never have been common: There is such an *unfortunate contrariety* in most of the Doctor's narratives, that he generally furnishes an antidote against the poison which he means to communicate.

Page 155, he talks of people " lying dead by families as they stood." *Lying as they stood* is a mode of expression which none but a *Lexicographer*, who can give to words what meaning he pleases, would venture to put upon paper. It would appear, from this accurate phrase, as if the Doctor intended to enrich the *English* language by supplies from the *Irish* establishment.

From an anxiety to annihilate, if possible, every vestige of antiquity in the Highlands, he is at much pains, in pages 160, 161, 162, to explain away a *Dun*, or Danish fort, of which there are many in the country, into a fence for securing cattle from thieves. This attempt is the more chimerical and absurd, as it cannot be conceived how so small an area, though much larger than he makes it, could contain such a number of cattle as would compensate the trouble of rearing it; and which, according to his own account of the matter, must have been very great.

The dimensions of this building, as stated by Dr. *Johnson*, are very erroneous. He says the area is but forty-two feet in diameter, and the height of the wall only about nine; but the fact is, that the former is seventy-two feet, and the latter about fifteen and upwards. So small a space, at best, could not have answered the purpose
assigned

assigned to it by the Doctor; but, according to his own measure, it would have been altogether useless. In those pastoral times, it could not contain the cattle of a single individual, who was of consequence enough to raise such a fabric; much less could it afford shelter for the stock of a whole clan, or a country.

The height is another argument against the Doctor's hypothesis. Even the nine feet, which he allows, were by far too much for a mere *fence from thieves*; as the half of that would have been fully sufficient. He is apt enough, at other times, to accuse the Highlanders of laziness and poverty. How, then, will he be able to account for so great a superfluity of labour and expence, when, instead of nine feet, the height is, at least, fifteen? A direct answer to this question must *puzzle* even Dr. *Johnson*; and it would certainly put any other man, in the same situation,

to

to something more than a difficulty—it would put him to the blush.

"The walls," he says, "are very thick." This likewise is against him, as a moderate degree of thickness would have been sufficient to resist the sudden incursions of freebooters. They never carried any levelling instruments, and they generally remained too short a time to overcome the strength of *very thick walls* by manual force alone.

Another, and perhaps not the least forcible objection to our Author's *idea*, is, that he tells us, "within the great circle were several smaller rounds of wall, which formed distinct apartments." *Ingenuity* itself must be at a loss to conceive how such a contrivance as this could have been devised for the more convenient stowage of cattle. But Dr. *Johnson* saves his reader the trouble of thinking long about the matter,

matter, and folves the difficulty by faying, that thefe interior apartments " were probably the fhelters of the keepers." This, I think, fettles the point at once. For, if the whole of the great circle is fubdivided into a number of fmaller chambers, which were occupied by the keepers, it is evident there could be no room for the cattle. The Doctor has with one ftroke of his pen overturned his own fyftem, and clearly proved againft himfelf, that the *Duns*, or *Towers*, fo frequent in the iflands, were intended as fhelters for *men*, and *not* for beafts.

Had he acquiefced in the natural account of this matter, which, he fays, was given him by Mr. Macqueen, it would have faved him all the trouble of framing an opinion of his own, as well as the *ridicule* of being at length obliged to abandon it as untenable.

The antiquity of thofe buildings cannot be exactly known; but it is highly probable that they are of *Danish* origin. They might have been used partly as fortresses, and partly as signal-houses, from which the *gok-man*, which in the Danish language signifies a *signal-man*, generally gave the alarm, and announced the approach of strangers either by sea or land.

Page 170, he says, the seas are commonly too rough in winter for nets, or boats, so that the inhabitants cannot fish. This assertion seems the more extraordinary, as he had said before, page 156, that while he was in the *Hebrides*, though the wind was extremely turbulent, he had never seen very high billows. Here, however, he had an hypothesis to support. He wanted to have another *stroke* at the poverty of the inhabitants; and therefore he found it necessary to make the sea stormy, that by depriving them of fish he might create a famine, as he flatly says, that other provision fails at that season. When the *good* Doctor has a

point

point of this nature to carry, he laughs at the restrictions of consistency and common sense.

Page 175, we find the Doctor at *Ostig* in *Sky*, where he was hospitably entertained for some days by Mr. *Martin Macpherson*, minister of *Slate*, and son to the late reverend and learned Dr. *John Macpherson*, formerly minister of the same parish.

As our traveller was now upon the spot where Dr. *Macpherson* had so long resided, and where he had so successfully employed his talents as a writer, one might naturally expect that he would have taken some opportunity of mentioning so distinguished a character with respect. By such a tribute to the memory of the father, he would have repaid the hospitality of the son in the most agreeable manner; while, at the same time, by doing justice to another's merit, he would have given a generous proof of his own candour and impartiality.

But, instead of that, the Doctor chuses to be silent; and we hear not a single word of Dr. *Macpherson* or his writings. This must certainly be owing to one or other of these causes, or to both; either to the jealousy of a little mind, which is incapable of conferring praise; or to our traveller's unwillingness to inform the public, that an author of such eminent abilities was a native of the Highlands.

Among other things, Dr. *Macpherson* had written professedly, and in a masterly manner, on the antiquities of his country: not from that tradition, which Dr. *Johnson* explodes, but, to use one of our traveller's expressions, from the " uncontaminated fountains of Greek and Roman literature." Where tradition completed the figure, of which the ancients drew the outlines,

outlines, Dr. *Macpherson* paid it that attention which it claims from writers whose object is truth; where it differed from incontestible authorities, he rejected it with proper contempt.

But it was not convenient for Dr. *Johnson*'s plan to mention even the name of a native of the Highlands, whose knowledge as a scholar, and elegance as an author, reflected so much honour on his country. As our dogmatical journalist wished to draw a veil over the history of our country, as well as over the genius of our countrymen, it would have been a species of *literary suicide* to have taken any notice of a writer whose industry and talents have placed the existence and truth of *both* beyond dispute. The directing his readers to Dr. *Macpherson*'s works, would infallibly pull down the fabulous fabric which Dr. *Johnson* intended to raise; and we must, therefore, commend his prudence,
whilst

whilst we exclude him from every pretence to candour.

Let me, therefore, tell the Doctor, that he would have done much greater justice to the public, as well as to Scotland, if, instead of trusting to his own *ingenuity* in many things, he had related the opinions of Dr. *Macpherson* and others. A few anecdotes from those authors would have been full as valuable to the purchasers of his book, as telling them, *that, one day, Mr. Boswell borrowed a boy's fishing-rod and caught a cuddy*; with a thousand other impertinent trifles of the same nature.

Page 183, in speaking of minerals, he says, " Common *ores* would be here of no great value; for what requires to be separated by fire must, if it were found, be carried away in its mineral state, here being no fuel for the smelting-house or forge."

forge." If this be true, how happens it that several English companies come to different parts of the *West* coast for charcoal, and bring *ore* all the way from England to be there smelted? Besides, it is well known that there is pit-coal in *Mull*; and, I am told, it is likewise to be had in one or more of the other islands.

Immediately after, he adds, " Perhaps, by diligent search in this world of stone, some valuable species of marble might be discovered. But neither philosophical curiosity nor commercial industry have yet fixed their abode here." Had our doughty *itinerant* himself carried any reasonable share of " philosophical curiosity" along with him, he might have observed abundance of white marble near *Corichattachan*, where he acknowledges he had been twice.

Page 186, he says, " The cattle go from the islands very lean, and are not offered

to

to the butcher till they have been long fatted in English pastures." The cattle that are sent from the islands are not generally so *very lean* when they set out, but they naturally become so before they are driven six or seven hundred miles. Were the fattest bullocks in England to travel in the same manner to the islands, they would probably not be very fit for being offered to the butcher when they arrived there. If the Doctor doubts the fact, let him drive a *live* stock before him, when he sets out on his next journey, and I will be answerable for the consequence.

Page 204, " The inhabitants," says he, " were for a long time perhaps not unhappy; but their content was a muddy mixture of pride and ignorance, an indifference for pleasures which they did not know, a blind veneration for their chiefs, and a strong conviction of their own importance." It may with more truth be said,

said, that this observation is a *muddy mixture* of a still less *honourable pride* and more *contemptible ignorance*; a total *indifference for truth*, if the contrary can but serve the turn; a *blind prejudice* against the whole *Scottish* nation; and a *strong conviction* in the Author's own mind, that he has here, as on many other occasions, most infamously and grossly *misrepresented* them.

As to our *pride*, he says in the following page, " Their pride has been crushed by the heavy hand of a vindictive conqueror." This is another retrospect to the year 1745. If ever the saying, that " *old men are twice children*," was verified by example, it is certainly on the present occasion. The peevish veteran has once taken it into his head to say, that the Scotch were then conquered, and he must be allowed to say so still, or there can be no peace with him. He therefore diverts himself with founding the horn of victory, as an overgrown *lubberly* boy would be pleafed with the noife of his *rattle*, or the blowing of his *whiftle*.

I have already endeavoured to place this matter in its proper light. I fhall now borrow a little of the Doctor's own affiftance to ftrengthen my arguments. Page 207, he fays, " To difarm part of the Highlands, could give no reafonable occafion of complaint. Every government muft be allowed the power of taking away the weapon that is lifted againft it. But the loyal clans murmured, with fome appearance of juftice, that, after having defended the king, they were forbidden for the future to defend themfelves; and that the fword fhould be forfeited, which had been legally employed. Their cafe is undoubtedly hard," &c.

Whoever reads this paffage will require little further proof, that the *idea* of a national

national conqueft is moft abfurd, and that the Doctor himfelf has furnifhed a decifive argument againft it. After this conceffion, could any one expect to hear him fay in the very fame page, " But the law, which followed the victory of Culloden, found the whole nation dejected and intimidated ?" He tells us in one place, that there were loyal clans, and that they defended the king. What occafion then had the whole nation to be *dejected* and *intimidated*, unlefs we can fuppofe that near two millions of people, who were innocent, were to be involved in the guilt of a few thoufands ? Such bare-faced contradictions are an anfwer to themfelves.

But let me tell the Doctor, that without the affiftance of the loyal clans he mentions, the victory of Culloden had never been heard of. Had he known, or rather adverted to this, I am perfuaded he would have been at lefs pains to celebrate an event,
wherein

wherein the *Scotch* themselves had more than an equal share.

The rebellion of 1745 was only a partial insurrection of a few discontented chiefs and their followers. Neither were those gentlemen the heads of the most numerous clans; nor did the whole of their respective tribes attend them to the field. Only nine parishes in the Highlands contributed a part of their inhabitants towards furnishing the rebel army. It would seem, however, that Dr. *Johnson*'s fears, and probably the fears of those about him at that time, had magnified the danger to a very high degree; and that may be one reason for his exalting the suppression of an inconsiderable tumult into a *splendid victory*. If the Doctor is not ashamed to confess his own panic, he ought not, for decency's sake, to have exposed *that* of his country.

That

That the infurgents met with little encouragement in Scotland, is evident. Their whole number amounted hardly to feven thoufand; and of thefe about two thoufand were *Englifh*. That a much greater proportion of our fouthern neighbours did not repair to the fame ftandard, was by no means owing to their poffeffing a greater fhare of loyalty. The difaffection of moft of their leading men, and the meafures they had concerted, are well known; they only waited for fome favourable moment to declare their intentions; in which, it muft be allowed, they fhewed themfelves much more prudent, if lefs refolute, than the Scotch.

He goes on to difcufs what he had afferted in page 204, as above quoted. Having " crufhed our pride by the heavy hand of a vindictive conqueror," in the manner we have feen, he comes next to expofe expose rather than to commiserate our ignorance.

Page 206, he says, "Their ignorance grows every day less, but their knowledge is yet of little other use than to shew them their wants." As to the first part of this *pompous* apophthegm, " that our ignorance grows every day less," I shall only observe, that if the same thing cannot be said of our friends the English, they must be a much duller people than I ever took them for. In regard to the second, he gives our knowledge its proper use. When people find out their wants, they will soon fall upon means to supply them. From the parade which accompanies this piece of intelligence, one would be apt, at first sight, to expect a great deal from it; but, when we examine it more narrowly, we shall find it only informs us, that as our knowledge becomes greater, our ignorance grows less.

But

But to be a little more serious with the Doctor, let me afk him, in what that ignorance confifted, which is fo *miraculoufly* growing lefs, by our learning to know more?

He feems to connect it with what he calls " an indifference for pleafures which we did not know." Does he mean the fafhionable pleafures of the *Englifh* metropolis? If he does, he has, at laft, paid us no fmall compliment. To make frequent vows at the fhrine of the voluptuous goddefs, is no great fign of the wifdom of any people. The puny fize and meagre form which mark out her votaries, afford no great temptation to follow their example.

I would gladly hope, however, that Dr. *Johnfon* is not a ferious advocate for intemperate pleafures; as it would give me a much worfe opinion of his morals, at leaft, than I would wifh to entertain.

Though he has been a *Rambler* in his younger days, he would certainly cut a bad figure as an old *Rake*. To say no worse, it would be ridiculous in the extreme to see such an *aggregate* of unfashioned matter "tottering, with paralytic stride, after sensual gratifications, and aukwardly assuming the light airs of modern libertinism."

I have already given several proofs that the Scotch were not behind their neighbours, either in useful or ornamental improvements, many centuries ago. I will now mention some other circumstances, to shew that the Doctor's charge of what he calls *ignorance* cannot apply to those times. To give his assertion weight, therefore, he ought to have told us when this national misfortune commenced, and wherein it now consists; for it must appear somewhat unaccountable, that the Scotch, who had once their full proportion of the improvements commonly known in Europe, should have

have made a retrograde motion, while other nations have been in a progressive state.

As to the state of learning among us, we have already seen how that matter stood in very early times. In particular, it has appeared from history, that St. *Aydan* and others were sent from *Scotland*, in the seventh century, to instruct some of the Doctor's countrymen in the first principles of Christianity. In succeeding times it must be allowed, that learning had considerably declined among our ancestors; but, even in that respect, the Scotch had only their share of the same *Gothic* cloud which, for a season, darkened the face of all Europe. This misfortune was owing every where to the Roman Catholic clergy, with whom it was an established maxim, that " *ignorance* was the *mother* of devotion." In mentioning the effect, therefore, the Doctor should have assigned the cause;

cause; but as that could not be done without a just censure on his favourite sect, he chuses to leave it behind the curtain. He takes such frequent opportunities of extolling the piety of monks, priests, and cardinals, that the dullest of his readers may easily discover his attachment to their tenets.

In regard to such arts and manufactures as were then commonly known over Europe, there are many proofs to shew, that they were anciently cultivated, not only in Scotland at large, but even in the *Hebrides*, in as great perfection as any where else. As to the islands in particular, I might venture to assert, that some ingenious arts, which were well understood by our forefathers, are now in a great measure lost, from that change in our modes of life which time and circumstances have introduced. This may appear a paradox to the Doctor, and perhaps to some others; but

I should

I should find no difficulty in proving it to be true, if such a discussion should appear to be necessary.

That a knowledge of the several arts must have been very generally disseminated over the Highlands, there can be no reason to doubt. It is well known that our kings resided often in that part of their dominions, as at Dunstaffnage, Dunmacsnichain, or Berigonium, Inverlochay, Inverness, and Logirate, &c. It is natural, therefore, to suppose, that they had at all those places a number of artists of all kinds, becoming their state and quality; and likewise, that the skill and knowledge of these men must necessarily be communicated to others. Several of the castles and magnificent palaces wherein the kings resided are still to be seen, though our traveller seems to have been determined to take no notice of them.

But though no king of Scotland had ever refided in the Highlands, our feveral chieftains lived in all the ftate of independent princes. Like the *feudal* lords of all other countries, they were often at variance with fome of their neighbours; and that rendered it abfolutely neceffary, that they fhould be provided with the means of every fpecies of accommodation, either for peace or war, within their own territories. This is another undeniable proof, that a very large proportion of the Highlanders muft have been well fkilled in the different arts.

There are yet many monuments of ancient mafonry among us, of different kinds, which greatly excel any thing of that nature in modern times. The curious hieroglyphics on fome of our tombs deferved particular notice, though Dr. *Johnfon* paffes over them in filence. Among other things, the huge maffes of ftone fet up up in druidical circles, particularly thofe fupported upon other ftones for druidical altars, and the obelifks erected in commemoration of battles, are demonftrable proofs of our knowledge of *mechanics*.

Many monuments of this kind are ftill to be feen, not only upon the continent or main-land of Scotland, but likewife in the iflands; though many others, within the memory of fome people ftill living, have been deftroyed to make way for the plough, or by other accidents. In particular, at *Inverliver* on the fide of Lochete, at *Glencetlen* in Glenete, in different parts in *Ifla*, and at *Callanis* and *Barvas* in the ifland of Lewis, there are maffes of fuch enormous fize and weight, as could not be raifed by any number of men that could ftand round them. *Clachan-an-Truifeil* near Barvas, particularly, is from two to two and a half feet thick, fix feet broad, and from feventeen to eighteen feet above ground.

As

As the stone stands in a *peat-moss*, or bog, there can be no less than a third part of it under ground; and it is probable there may be more. There are no stones or quarry of the same kind nearer to it than the sea-side, from which it stands about half a mile, on the ascent of a steep hill, and having a deep bog between.

In the island called from *O'Chormaic*, on the coast of *Knapdale*, and I think on the north-east side, there is a small commodious harbour, a great part of which is surrounded with a wall or quay, extremely well built; and the foundation of it is so deep, that it cannot be seen even at low water. What is remarkable of this is, that it is so old that no one pretends to know, even by tradition, when or by whom it was built.

The *Fletchers* of Glenlyon, in Perthshire, were the most famous *arrow-makers* of their time, so long as that weapon continued to be used.

The smelting and working of *iron* was well understood, and constantly practised, over all the Highlands and Islands for time immemorial. Instead of improving in that art, we have fallen off exceedingly of late years, and at present make little or none. Tradition bears, that they made it in the *blomary* way; that is, by laying it under the hammers, in order to make it malleable with the same heat that melted it in the furnace.

There is still in the Highlands a clan of the name of *Mac Nuithear*, who are descended from those founders, and have from thence derived their surname. I am likewise well informed, that there is in *Glenurchy*, in Argyleshire, a family of the name of *Mac Nab*, who have lived in the same place, and have been a race of smiths,

from

from father to fon, for more, perhaps, than three hundred years paſt; and who, in confequence of the father having inſtructed the fon, have carried down fo much of their ancient art, that they excel all others in the country, in the way of their profeſſion; even thofe taught in the fouth of Scotland, as well as in England, not excepted. A tinker or fmith of the name of *Mac Feadearan*, a tribe now almoſt extinct, was the moſt famous of his time for making arrow-heads.

It is certain that *Mac Donald* was formerly poſſeſſed of moſt of the *weſtern* iſles, as well as of feveral large diſtricts upon the continent or main-land. He had many places of refidence, fuch as *Ardtoriniſh*, &c.; but the moſt common one was in an iſland in Lochfinlagan in *Iſla*. Near this place, and not far from *Port Aſkaic* on the found of Iſla, lived the fmith *Mac Cregie* (that is, the fon of the Rock), and his

his posterity for a great length of time. There is still pointed out, by the inhabitants, the rock out of which he dug his *iron ore*. Near the rock is a large solid stone, of a very hard consistency, on which he knapped his ore; and, at a little distance, there is a cascade on a rivulet, where stood his mill for polishing, or otherwise preparing the iron which he had manufactured. Here he and his descendents made complete suits of armour, according to the fashion of the times; such as helmets, swords, coats of mail, &c. The *Isla* hilt for the broad sword is well known, and so famous as to have become proverbial.

As to our *navigation*, there is reason to believe that it bore a near proportion to that of our neighbours: sea-engagements with *Birlins* were very common in the Highlands till of late. Lymphad, or Galley, was the same with *Longh-fhad* (Long-ship), or Birlin.

There

There was a ship of war built in Scotland, in the minority of James IV. the equal of which had never been built in Britain, nor seen upon the seas in those times. Its dimensions I am not just now able to ascertain; but they have been accurately described by several of our historians, whom I have not at present an opportunity of consulting.

In 1490, *Andrew Wood*, with two Scots ships, took five ships belonging to the English, though much superior to his own in size. With the same two ships he afterwards took three English ships, the best that could be picked out of *Henry* the Eighth's whole fleet, and equipped for the purpose. They were commanded by *Stephen Bull*, as admiral, the only man in England that could be found to undertake the expedition; and they had the further advantage of being clean out of the dock,

while

while *Wood* had been some time upon a cruise on the coast of Holland, and totally ignorant of the trap that was intended for him on his return.

From this the Doctor may perceive, that we could and did cope with the *formidable* fleets of England, and even obtained signal advantages over them, at a time long prior to that in which he continues to represent us as a nation of *ignorant* savages and barbarians.

With respect to *carpentry*, or joiner's work, we have still many specimens, in oak, of very high antiquity, which greatly excel any thing that is done by modern artists.

Our shields, or *targets*, likewise, consisting of wood, leather, and often a plate of steel, with regularly placed and polished

brass

brafs ftuds, which fometimes formed different figures and reprefentations of things, prove, beyond a doubt, that we had people very early who could work with dexterity in a variety of materials.

Many more inftances might be given; but thofe above, I flatter myfelf, will be fufficient to convince the Doctor, though perhaps he may not confefs it, that such arts as were known to other nations, were not at any period of time unknown in Scotland. The *Englifh* are but too apt to claim a fuperiority, in moft things, over all their neighbours; but we know perfectly well, that they can boaft but of few inventions, and that they are not over remarkable for making quick improvements on the inventions of others. But I wifh not, by any means, to launch into general reflections, for the indifcretion of Dr. *Johnfon* and a few others.

We

We are fully satisfied ourselves, and so, we hope, are others, that it is not our ignorance or want of genius that has brought such a deluge of falsehood and abuse upon us from our worthy traveller. It is something else, which he himself thinks the reverse of these, that has provoked so much asperity; and we hope we shall always continue to furnish him with the same reasons for jealousy and detraction. We wish not that Dr. *Johnson* should ever speak of us in a different style. As his pride and envy know no bounds, he is seldom obliging where others would confer applause. His censure, therefore, implies a claim to merit.

In a long string of quaint axioms, he tells us, page 211, " That the martial character cannot prevail in a whole people, but by the diminution of all other virtues." By this, he endeavours to rob the Highlanders of every thing that is valuable, but their bravery. He could devise no means to deprive them of that, and therefore he was resolved to leave them no other qualification. But, in aiming this thrust at the Scotch, he seems not aware what **a deep** wound he gives to *Old* England at the same time. His own countrymen will not easily give up their claim to the *martial character*; and yet, I believe, they would not chuse to confirm the Doctor's reasoning, by renouncing their pretensions to *all other virtues*. The French, Germans, and Swiss, are all allowed to possess the martial character; but their politeness, humanity, and other virtues cannot be called in question. Among individuals, it has commonly been observed, that the most cowardly were always the most cruel and barbarous. I thought likewise that the same maxim had been established in regard to nations; and I must think so still, till something stronger has appeared against it than has been advanced by Dr. *Johnson*.

When

When a man is at variance with the common sense of mankind, his opinions may, at first, surprise a little by their novelty; but the surprise excited by impudent singularity is soon followed by contempt.

In the same and the following page, he says, " Every provocation was revenged with blood, and no man that ventured into a numerous company, by whatever occasion brought together, was sure of returning without a wound." What the Doctor says here is, so far, very right. No man certainly could be sure of any thing that was to happen, without the gift of *prescience*; but there was a much greater probability of a man returning safe, in the case he states, than that an inhabitant of *London*, after going to bed, shall not have his house robbed, or his throat cut, before next morning.

Different interests, as happened in all other countries, under the feudal institution, made different clans sometimes interfere with one another. The same causes, I believe, are attended with similar effects in most parts of England, even in this refined age. There are few contested elections, I am told, without producing tumult, disorder, danger, and sometimes death. In regard to those of the same clan, at the time alluded to, they not only lived peaceably together, but likewise in the most friendly manner; and generally with less design upon each other than, I am afraid, is to be found among some people who consider themselves as much more civilised. Were the Doctor's representation of the country just, it must certainly have been long since depopulated.

Page 213, he says, " The power of deciding controversies, and of punishing offences, as some such power there must

always

always be, was entrusted to the lairds of the country, to those whom the people confidered as their natural judges. It cannot be fuppofed that a rugged proprietor of the rocks, unprincipled and unenlightened, was a nice refolver of entangled claims, or very exact in proportioning punifhment to offences." To make good his point, the Doctor here takes fomething for granted.

Why fhould he fuppofe the lairds to be *unprincipled*, though fome of them might happen, now and then, to be fomewhat *unenlightened* in the intricate points of law? In matters of equity, which were the only queftions that could come before them, and thefe by a reference from both the parties, a man of a good underftanding and folid fenfe might not make a bad arbiter; and Highlanders in general have not been reckoned deficient in a reafonable fhare of fagacity. Thofe whom the Doctor calls

calls *nice refolvers of entangled claims*, are often as great *confounders* of plain cafes.

But the Doctor's obfervations on the mode of diftributing juftice among the Highlanders muft fall to the ground, as they are not founded upon matter of fact. The chiefs never fat as judges, either in civil or criminal cafes. The conftitution of the Highlands, if the expreffion may be ufed, was exactly the fame with that of all other countries, where the feudal fyftem of government prevailed. The chief, as proprietor of the land, nominated a judge to decide upon differences between his tenants. In matters of property, there lay an appeal to the King's courts in a regular gradation.

In criminal cafes, though the culprit was tried in the diftrict where the crime was committed, a jury was fummoned from the whole county, and formed in the fame juft just and unexceptionable manner as is practised at present by the High Court of Justiciary in Scotland. The jurymen did not consist, as I am informed they frequently do in the Doctor's country, of low and *unenlightened* tradesmen and mechanics. On the contrary, they were men of landed property in the county; all gentlemen of consequence and consideration, who had a character to lose by any deviation from the established maxims of justice; of which, as they are imprinted on the human mind, the bulk of mankind are judges in every country. The number of the jurymen, likewise, was always greater in Scotland than in England; which was an additional security for justice.

The Doctor makes some amends for what he had so rashly asserted, in the next paragraph. "When the chiefs," adds he, "were men of knowledge and virtue, the convenience of a domestic judicature was great. No long journies were necessary, no artificial delays could be practised; the character, the alliances, and interests of the litigants were known to the court, and all false pretences were easily detected. The sentence, when it was past, could not be evaded; the power of the laird superseded formalities, and justice could not be defeated by interest or stratagem." Here he speaks with more decency, though he is still wrong in the principle.

Page 215. " The roads are secure in those places, through which, forty years ago, no traveller could pass without a convoy." To borrow a little of his own *polite* language, it may justly be said here, that the Doctor is either " *unprincipled*" or " *unenlightened.*" His information, if he had any, was certainly very bad; and if he speaks at hazard, the infamy of his misrepresentation is apparent.

I am sorry when the Doctor obliges me to draw comparisons between the two kingdoms;

doms; but I must inform him, that the Highlanders never lurked on the public roads to disturb ordinary travellers, like the banditti who at present infest all the roads in England. A robbery or murder was always a rare thing in the Highlands. Even in the rudest times our ancestors disdained such practices; it is not therefore probable, that the present generation should be less civilised than their forefathers.

Whatever hostilities they committed, it was always openly and avowedly; and only by way of reprisal on those with whom they were at enmity. The most polite nations in Europe take still the same advantages, when in a state of war with their neighbours. When therefore two clans were at variance, it might happen, indeed, that those belonging to either of them might sometimes find it convenient to travel in larger parties than usual for security, especially

cially if their route led them near the territories of the other.

If the Doctor's *convoy* was not of this fort, I am at a lofs to find it out. I never heard of any other; and even the neceffity of that did not come fo far down as he ftates it. In any other cafe, a fingle traveller might pafs from one end of the country to the other unmolefted, and with much lefs danger of infult or depredation than even in *Fleet-ftreet*, where, I am told, the *pure* Dr. *Johnfon* has not difdained to fix his abode.

In the very next fentence of the fame page, he fays, "All trials of right by the fword are forgotten." This mode of deciding points of right would, I confefs, have been a reproach to our forefathers, had it been only in ufe among them. But as the fame kind of appeal prevailed in *England*, and other European countries, at
the

the fame time, it is rather fomewhat *little* in this *great* man to exhibit that cuftom now, as a characteriftic of the ancient Highlanders.

Page 227, he obferves, " England has for feveral years been filled with the atchievements of feventy thoufand Highlanders employed in *America*. I have heard from an Englifh officer, not much inclined to favour them, that their behaviour deferved a very high degree of military praife; but their number has been much exaggerated. One of the minifters told me, that feventy thoufand men could not have been found in all the Highlands, and that more than twelve thoufand never took the field." The number faid to have been employed in America, if the Doctor ever heard fuch a report, was certainly much exaggerated. No more than about five thoufand were employed on the American fervice; and thofe were only the
Royal

Royal Highlanders, with *Frazer*'s and *Montgomery*'s regiments. The former consisted of two battalions of eleven hundred each; and each of the latter had fourteen hundred men. They did not act in a body together; every corps had a separate destination.

Though there were not seventy thousand Highlanders employed in America, nor indeed in the whole service, there were certainly more than that number of men raised in Scotland, during the course of the last war; but a large proportion of these were *Lowlanders*; and they, likewise, did much honour to the British arms, as well as to their native country. The Doctor, however, makes the Scotch levies all Highlanders, and sends the whole seventy thousand to America, as he could not allow the *atchievements* of which he had heard to five thousand only. This furnishes an equal proof of his admiration and envy.

As the Doctor is never long of one mind, he foon veers about, and reduces his feventy thoufand to twelve. He fays he was told by one of the minifters, that feventy thoufand men could not be found in all the Highlands, and that more than twelve thoufand never took the field.

The Doctor, on more occafions than one, feems to have been much indebted to the Scotch clergy for intelligence; at leaft, he often adduces them as vouchers for what he fays. It is remarkable, however, that when he makes ufe of their teftimony for any thing that derogates from the importance of the country, he always conceals their names. This has a very fufpicious look, as we have no direction for inveftigating the fact; and none of thofe gentlemen can find himfelf refponfible to refute an anonymous charge.

I will

I will allow the Doctor, if he pleases, that seventy thousand men could not easily be found in the Highlands, to enter the service all at one time; and, I believe, it might even distress *Old England* itself to furnish an equal number of efficient recruits on a sudden emergency. But I will deny that no more than twelve thousand Highlanders were employed in our different armies, in the course of the last war; and I will be bold to aver, that no minister ever gave him the information he pretends. There is not a minister in Scotland, much less in the Highlands, but knows the contrary. There were, at one time, fifteen battalions of Highlanders, distinguished by their native dress; which may be reckoned at sixteen thousand men at least: for if two or three of those corps, and I am sure there were no more, fell a little short of their full complement of a thousand each, all the rest had a surplus much more than sufficient to make up the deficiency.

In

In this there can be no deception. Whoever has curiosity enough, may have recourse to the *War-office* for a confirmation of the fact. Besides, it is certain, that many more than the number I have just now mentioned, were dispersed through other regiments, without any external distinction as Highlanders. We had constantly recruiting parties among us, and they seldom beat up without finding volunteers.

Hence we find that our author is not more lucky in the stories which he palms upon others, than in the fidelity of his own observations; but he does not always deal in anonymous authority. He professedly places some things to Mr. *Boswell's* account, which I am sorry to see. Had I therefore an opportunity of meeting that gentleman, I would certainly ask him, whether his fellow-traveller, Dr. *Samuel Johnson*, had not taken improper liberties with

with his name? and if he avowed the facts, I would not hesitate to tell him, that, if he had not ignorance for an excuse, he had shewn little regard to candour.

As to the English officer, who professed himself not much inclined to favour the Highlanders, but owned that their behaviour deserved a very high degree of military praise, the Doctor has done him a kindness in suppressing his name. If known, he could hardly have accounted to the world for so strange an antipathy; and though concealed, if he has lived to see the *Journey to the Hebrides*, and recollects himself in the above passage, he must feel somewhat aukwardly in his own mind. To avow a dislike, and to acknowledge a claim to praise at the same time, exceeds even the usual extravagance of *English* prejudice.

Page 230, he fays, " The traveller, who comes hither from more opulent countries, to fpeculate upon the remains of paftoral life, will not much wonder that a common Highlander has no ftrong adherence to his native foil." The attachment of Scotchmen in general, and of Highlanders in particular, to their native country, has always been remarkable, even to a degree of enthufiafm; which certainly would not have been the cafe, were that country as deftitute of comfortable enjoyments as the Doctor often reprefents it. He is here confuted by the general voice of his own countrymen, who daily upbraid the Scotch for their national adherence. His affertion, therefore, muft lofe credit on both hands. The Highlander will fpurn the malignant infinuation with contempt; and no Englifhman will believe it.

But as Dr. *Johnfon* will prove the moft unexceptionable evidence againft himfelf, I fhall

I shall to this paſſage oppoſe another from his own work. When he was leaving *Anoch* in Glenmorriſon, where he had ſtaid a night, and was ſo much captivated with the genteel appearance and behaviour of his landlord's daughter, he tells us, that their hoſt, when they left his houſe in the morning, walked by them a great way, and entertained them with converſation both on his own condition and that of the country. " From him," continues he, page 79, " we firſt heard of the general diſſatisfaction (the raiſing of the rents), which is now driving the Highlanders into the other hemiſphere; and when I aſked him whether they would ſtay at home, if they were well treated, he anſwered with indignation, that no man willingly left his native country." This, I preſume, will be deemed a ſufficient comment upon the preceding quotation.

It

It is not the first time we have seen the Doctor's narrations at *cross purposes* with each other. We can account for his misrepresentations from his prejudices; his contradictions, however, will require a different solution. A badness of heart may induce a man to calumniate others; but there is a degree of insanity in exposing one's own shame.

Page 238. We have here another of our traveller's inconsistencies. " The general conversation of the Islanders," says he, " has nothing particular. I did not meet with the inquisitiveness of which I have read, and suspect the judgment to have been rashly made." How will this be reconciled with what he has said before in page 116, where he describes the same people as full of curiosity and of the love of talk?

But the cafe is fo very different from what the Doctor alleges in this place, that the inquifitivenefs of the common people in the Highlands has been generally thought to border upon a good-natured kind of officioufnefs. I do not mention this as a circumftance very much to be applauded; but it is harmlefs at leaft, and fhews that the Doctor has formed a wrong eftimate of that part of their character, if he ftates the matter as he really found it. Many of them, however, for want of his language, might be unable to exprefs their curiofity, let it be ever fo great.

As to the better fort, they were always very delicate in their inquiries, as the Doctor's anfwers were generally rude and unmannerly. While in the Hebrides, he was for the moft part fo fulky and ill-humoured, that even their affiduities to pleafe him feemed to give offence. It may naturally be supposed, therefore, that a people always remarkable for their politeness to strangers, would be very shy in obtruding any thing that might prove disagreeable to their guest. When the Doctor was in a mood for conversation, they heard him with attention, and answered his questions with civility; but, with all that *curiosity* and *love of talk*, which he has allowed them in another place, they seldom ventured to solicit him for any information in return. The natural roughness of his manners was sometimes so excessive, that he even treated the ladies with disrespect; and nothing but a regard to the laws of hospitality prevented the gentlemen often from shewing marks of their displeasure.

Page 239. " There are now parochial schools, to which the lord of every manor pays a certain stipend. Here the children are taught to read; but, by the rule of their

their inftitution, they teach only *Englifh*, fo that the natives read a language which they may never ufe or underftand." The Doctor undertakes to give too much information for the fhort ftay he made in the *Hebrides*. The time could not allow a proper inveftigation of fo many particulars, were he more difpofed to be faithful in his accounts; and therefore it is no wonder that we fo often find him miftaken.

Here he evidently confounds the *parochial* with the *charity* fchools. The former are provided with falaries in the manner he mentions; but the latter are fupported by royal bounty. There has not been a parifh in Scotland for fome centuries without a parochial fchool; and every thing within the compafs of the mafter's knowledge, who is always a man of univerfity education, is regularly taught. There is no prohibition againft teaching any thing,

not

not even the *Gaelic*, so much the Doctor's abhorrence, excepted; though, at the same time, that is not a branch of education in those seminaries.

The *charity* schools are of much later institution; and, being intended originally for the poorer sort, the children pay no fees. The same qualifications are not requisite in the masters of these. They chiefly teach English, writing, and arithmetic; though several of them teach book-keeping likewise in so great perfection as to fit the youth under their care for the counting-house. By their first institution, it is true, they were prohibited to teach the *Gaelic*; but the impropriety of that prohibition struck the managers so forcibly afterwards, that in their next instructions they altered that clause, and gave orders for teaching it.

Page 240. In *Sky*, he says, " The scholars are birds of passage, who live at school only in the summer; for in winter provisions cannot be made for any considerable number in one place. This periodical dispersion impresses strongly the scarcity of these countries." It may with more justice be said, that this account of the matter *impresses much more strongly* the author's uniform intention of misrepresenting facts. The very reverse of what he here says is true; for the schools over all the Highlands are much more frequented in winter than in summer. I have already had occasion to mention, that the winter is far from being a season of scarcity in the Hebrides; as the people, by that kind of providence which is common to all mankind, prepare for it in due time. Nor is the absence of several of the scholars in summer owing to the *illiberal* cause assigned by Dr. *Johnson*, as affecting the winter. The children of the

less

less opulent sort of people, who are fit for domestic services, are more wanted in that season at home.

Page 242. The Islanders, says he, " have no reason to complain of insufficient pastors; for I saw not one in the islands whom I had reason to think either deficient in learning or irregular in life; but found several with whom I could not converse without wishing, as my respect increased, that they had not been Presbyterians." A few lines after he goes on, " The ministers in the islands had attained such knowledge as may justly be admired in men who have no motive to study, but generous curiosity, or, what is still better, desire of usefulness; with such politeness as so narrow a circle of converse could not have supplied, but to minds naturally disposed to elegance."

Some regard to truth and candour has prevailed for once. But notwithstanding
these

these generous effusions, for which some acknowledgments are due to the Doctor, let me ask him, how this account of the Highland clergy, for their learning and politeness, accords with what he says, in page 376, of our Scotch education? Speaking there of the universities of Scotland, he declares, that " men bred in them obtain only a mediocrity of knowledge, between learning and ignorance." As none of those gentlemen were bred any where else, it will readily occur to the reader, that such opposite accounts of the Highland ministers and the Scotch colleges cannot be both true. He will therefore judge for himself which to reject.

But whatever respect Dr. *Johnson* had for the ministers as men, he seems to have no charity for them as *Presbyterians*. His confession on that head may serve as a key to many other things, and shews that much justice and impartiality is not to be expected

from

from a man who is not ashamed to own such prejudices. The compliment to the ministers, therefore, ends in a satire upon himself.

In the same page he says, he " met with prejudices sufficiently malignant among the Presbyterians, but they were prejudices of ignorance." As he does not specify the nature of those prejudices, no reply can be made. His disposition, I believe, was *sufficiently malignant* to have pointed them out, had there been any that could have served his purpose. By being particular, a man assumes an air of truth at least; but a general assertion will not do, at this time of day, from Dr. *Johnson*. We have already seen too much laxity in his observations to give him credit for more than he is able to render probable, if not to prove. But while the *good* Doctor talks of malignant prejudices among the Presbyterians, as being the effects of ignorance,

let

let me civilly afk him, if he muft *not* be fufpected of ignorance, to what more dignified caufe we are to impute thofe *malignant prejudices* of his own, which have difgraced almoft every page of his work?

Page 245. " There is in Scotland, as among ourfelves, a reftlefs fufpicion of popifh machinations, and a clamour of numerous converts to the Romifh religion. The report is, I believe, in both parts of the ifland equally falfe. The Romifh religion is profeffed only in *Egg* and *Canna*, two fmall iflands, into which the Reformation never made its way. If any miffionaries are bufy in the Highlands, their zeal entitles them to refpect, even from thofe who cannot think favourably of their doctrine."

We have here a frefh and very ftriking inftance of the Doctor's attachment to the Romifh religion. He affects to difbelieve the

the reports of numerous converts being made, left people should take the alarm, and put a stop to the practice; and he concludes the passage with a very curious argument in favour of toleration. No one, I believe, will doubt *his* respect for popish missionaries; but how their zeal, in propagating their tenets, should entitle them to respect from those who disapprove of them, is something beyond my comprehension.

In confining the Romish religion in the Highlands to *Egg* and *Canna* only, he must be either ignorant or insincere. It is somewhat surprising, indeed, that a man, who, as he terms it himself, came purposely " to speculate upon the country," should return so very ill informed in a matter of so much consequence. Had he taken a little more pains, he must have heard, that there were many of the *Romish religion* in Strath-glafs, Brae-mar, Lochaber, and Glengary; and that the inhabitants

bitants of Cnoideart, Muideart, Arafaig, Morthair, South-Uift, and Barra, in all a vaft extent of country, are Roman catholics almoft to a man.

This is a more juft ftate of the fact than what has been given by the Doctor. He will not, I fuppofe, be difpleafed to hear it; and I am forry I cannot help giving him the further pleafure of affuring him, that the *Romifh religion* has been confiderably upon the growing hand in all the three kingdoms for feveral years paft.

Page 246, he fays, "The ancient fpirit that appealed only to the fword is yet among the Highlanders." This furely muft appear a bold affertion, after telling us before, in page 128, "That the military ardour of the Highlanders was extinguifhed," and ftill more directly, in page 215, "That all trials of right by the fword are forgotten." When the Doctor has

has a turn to serve, he throws out at random whatever suits him best; and when another purpose requires a different account of the very same matter, he is not over scrupulous about altering his detail. The poor Highlanders must be moulded into all shapes, to conform with his views. At one time, we see them an abject and *dispirited* race of men; at another, they swagger in all the *savage* pride of their " *ancient ferocity.*"

When we meet with such gross and palpable contradictions, it would be a mild construction *only* to suppose that the Doctor sometimes forgets what he has said before. This is as far as charity can go. But the writer who needs our charity is in a more contemptible situation than the wretch who lives by it.

In page 248, our traveller comes to examine the question of the *second sight*; and it is truly furprifing to fee with what a credulous weaknefs he endeavours to defend fo vifionary an opinion. Other things, which are believed by every man in the country, which are probable in themfelves, and are fupported by all the evidence that a reafonable man could expect, the Doctor often rejects; but this point, abfurd in itfelf, uncountenanced by any decent authority, and to which only a few of the moſt ignorant vulgar give the leaſt faith, he maintains with a zeal which ſhews him to be afhamed of nothing but thinking like other men.

In attempting to define the *fecond fight*, he feems to be much at a lofs. In page 149, he calls it a faculty, for power, he fays, it cannot be called; and yet, in page 154, he veers about again, and calls the *fecond fight* of the *Hebrides* a power.

If

If there is any real distinction between a faculty and a power, it would appear, from this variation of language, that the Doctor has not been able to find it out.

His reasonings upon the subject, for they cannot be called arguments, may amuse some readers, but they can convince none. They are too obscure to be understood by the illiterate, and they want strength to impress men of knowledge. But though our peregrinator has not been ashamed to exhibit his own superstitious credulity, it is a daring piece of insolence to introduce the names of a *Bacon* and a *Boyle* to give credit to such ridiculous nonsense.

Such a faculty or power, or whatever the Doctor pleases to call it, must always have depended, if ever it existed, upon some superior agency, and consequently must have been excited at particular times for some good purposes. We can see no adequate reason, therefore, for the *second sight* being local; and still less, if possible, for its being confined to the lower ranks of people. To have answered the intention of such a gift, it ought to have been general,—in *China*, and at the *Land's End*, as well as in the *Hebrides*,—and conferred upon the rich and the learned, as well as upon the poor and the ignorant.

In support of the *second sight*, Dr. Johnson uses only two particular arguments, if they deserve that name, which seem worthy of any notice. In page 254, he says, " Where we are unable to decide by antecedent reason, we must be content to yield to the force of testimony." This, in general, is certainly a very just observation, and worthy of a better subject. Had the Doctor always applied it in cases where a rational testimony was to be obtained, he would have been entitled to that claim

to

to candour which he has so often forfeited.

His next plea is as follows: in the same page he says, " By pretension to *second sight*, no profit was ever sought or gained. It is an involuntary affection, in which neither hope nor fear are known to have any part. Those who profess to feel it, do not boast of it as a privilege, nor are considered by others as advantageously distinguished. They have no temptation to feign, and their hearers have no motive to encourage the imposture."

Here the Doctor is evidently under a very gross mistake. Whatever he may think, if he really writes as he thinks, it is a well known fact, that those who have pretended to the *second sight* always considered it as a peculiar distinction, of which they were not a little vain; and it is no less true, that such as were weak enough to pay any regard to their pretensions were always afraid of offending, and desirous of pleasing them, as believing they had a communication with a superior order of beings. Whether the artful might not find here a temptation for imposture, I shall leave the reader to judge.

If this faculty, power, or affection, had ever any existence, except in the presumption of the designing or the imagination of the credulous, it is now visibly upon the decline, without any loss to the country; and it is to be hoped a few years more will extinguish the very memory of so great a reproach to the human understanding. In proportion as the light of knowledge has dawned upon mankind, their eagerness for wonders and belief in supernatural endowments have gradually abated. We may, therefore, naturally expect that the *second sight* of the *Hebrides*

will

will soon share the same fate with the late *witchcrafts* of Old England.

The Doctor says, that one of the ministers told him that he came to *Sky* with a resoution not to believe the *second sight*; a declaration which he shews a willingness to censure, as implying an unreasonable degree of incredulity. But as our traveller seems to have gone to *Sky* with a resolution to believe nothing else, we shall leave the merits of his *credulity* in this case, and *incredulity* in all others, with the impartial public.

I shall now dismiss this subject, as unworthy of any further discussion, and permit Dr. *Johnson*, with all his *pretensions* to philosophy, to believe the *second sight* as long as he pleases. It is a harmless delusion, and can hurt nobody. Some minds have a stronger propensity to superstition than others; and there is the less reason to be surprised at this instance of it in the Doctor, that I am told he was one of those *wise* men who sat up whole nights, some years ago, repeating *paternosters* and other *exorcisms*, amidst a group of old women, to conjure the *Cock-lane* ghost.

Our traveller next proceeds to other observations. In pages 256 and 257, he says, " As there subsists no longer in the islands much of that peculiar and discriminative form of life, of which the idea had delighted our imagination, we were willing to listen to such accounts of past times as would be given us; but we soon found what memorials were to be expected from an illiterate people, whose whole time is a series of distress; where every morning is labouring with expedients for the evening; and where all mental pains or pleasure arose from the dread of winter, the expectations of spring, the caprices of their chiefs, and the motions of the neighbouring

ing clans; where there was neither shame from ignorance, nor pride from knowledge; neither curiosity to inquire, nor vanity to communicate."

Were this representation of the Islanders true, it is certainly a very dismal one. But it is always some consolation to the miserable, to find others in no better a situation than themselves. Let us compare this account with what he gives us, a little before, of the human race in general. In page 250, he says, " Good seems to have the same proportion in those visionary scenes, as it obtains in real life: almost all remarkable events have evil for their basis, and are either miseries incurred, or miseries escaped. Our sense is so much stronger of what we suffer, than of what we enjoy, that the ideas of pain predominate in almost every mind. What is recollection but a revival of vexations,—or history, but a record of wars, treasons, and calamities?

Death, which is confidered as the greateft evil, happens to all. The greateft good, be it what it will, is the lot but of a part."

Here is exhibited a picture of human life more ghaftly than the *Gorgon*'s head, and fufficient to chill every breaft with horror. We may naturally confider the Doctor, while he wrote in this manner, to have been actuated by a deep fit of melancholy and defpair; and what he fays of the Iflanders fo foon afterwards, feems to have been dictated under the remains of the fame gloomy paroxyfm. Thofe who find an exact reprefentation of their own ftate in the general portrait of mifery here given, can have no reafon to contemplate the inhabitants of the iflands as diftin-guifhed by peculiar calamities. But fuch as can perceive no fimilitude of themfelves in that *frightful* group (and it is to be hoped there are many), will be naturally difpofed disposed to make some allowance for an extraordinary dash of colouring in the Doctor's account of the *Hebrides*.

Though the matter might be suffered to rest here, it may be worth while to examine the *rhapsody* of our traveller, concerning the Islanders, somewhat more minutely. I shall therefore beg the Doctor's leave to analyse that *remarkable* paragraph; that by contrasting its several parts separately, with what he has advanced on other occasions, we may the better determine what degree of credit he can claim from the public. As he is to be weighed in his own balance, he will have himself only to blame, if—" *he is found wanting.*"

" We soon found what memorials were to be expected from an illiterate people." His panegyric on the learning and politeness of the Highland *clergy* has been already

already observed: in page 119, he acknowledges that he never was in any house of the islands, where he did not find books in more languages than one; adding, in the beginning of the next page, that *literature* is not neglected by the higher rank of the Hebridians: and, from what he says of the *inn-keeper* at Anoch, and others of the same class, it is evident that he often found an unexpected degree of education in the intermediate spheres of life.

With what confidence then can Dr. *Johnson* talk of an illiterate people? So indiscriminate a charge is certainly intended to be understood as general; but if there is any truth in himself, it cannot appear to be just. He has admitted learning among the Islanders, where a man of sense and candour would expect to find it any where else; and to insinuate that it goes no further, if that really be his meaning, is but giving a fresh proof of his own absurdity.

absurdity. He has, therefore, no other alternative. He must either stand convicted of insincerity in his accounts of the higher and middle ranks of men, or he must confine the appellation of *illiterate* to the very lowest of the people. If he chuses the latter, he can derive no great credit from the remark he makes; as it appears from his own words, that it was among this order only that he sought for what he calls memorials.

In that case, it is no great wonder if he was often disappointed. But that can be deemed no peculiar reproach to the inferior inhabitants of the islands, till the Doctor proves that every cottager in *England* is a man of letters, and capable of satisfying the curiosity of a traveller in the nicest points of inquiry.

" Every morning is labouring with expedients for the evening." This is a proof of their induſtry at leaſt, in contradiction to that *lazineſs* and *averſion to labour*, with which the Doctor ſo often upbraids them in other places. That the time preſent ſhould labour for the future can appear nothing remarkable, as we generally find it to be the great buſineſs of life in every country whatever. We, therefore, can ſee nothing here to find fault with, unleſs it be that Dr. *Johnſon* was angry becauſe thoſe *ſavages* and *barbarians*, as he frequently calls them, were as wiſe and provident as their neighbours.

" All mental pains or pleaſure ariſe from the dread of winter, the expectation of ſpring, the caprices of their chiefs, and the motions of the neighbouring clans."

There has been occaſion to ſhew, more than once, that the winter is not ſo very dreadful a ſeaſon in the *Hebrides*, as our traveller

traveller represents it. I shall therefore refer this part of the argument to the reader's recollection of what has been already said.

As to the evils to be apprehended from the caprices of the chiefs, the Doctor himself is kind enough, as on most other occasions, to help me out with an answer. He takes frequent opportunities to observe, that the patriarchal authority of the chiefs is, in a great measure, abolished; but I shall only take notice of what he says in pages 205 and 215.

In the former of these he tells us, "That the chiefs being now deprived of their jurisdiction, have already lost much of their influence, and that they are in a fair way of being soon divested of the little that remains." Whether this be true or not, is of little consequence in the present question; it is sufficient to shew that the

Doctor is inconsistent with himself.—In the last-mentioned page, after comparing the present with ancient times, he says, " that now, however, there is happily an end to all fear or hope from malice or from favour;" and a little after, " that the mean are in as little danger from the powerful as in other places."

If the Doctor has not been mistaken in these observations, I would ask him, on what foundation he now builds the caprices of the chiefs?

The motions of the neighbouring clans ceased with the jurisdictions and other prerogatives of the chiefs. The Doctor is sufficiently sensible of this change, and is at abundant pains, in other places, to shew by what means it was effected; though, in his usual way, having a particular purpose to answer at this time, he is resolved to keep up the old custom.

A passage

A passage or two from himself will discover, whether he has always given reason to believe that there is now any cause of dread from the motions of the neighbouring clans. In page 206, he says, " The chief has lost his formidable retinue; and the Highlander walks his heath unarmed and defenceless, with the peaceable submission of a French peasant or English cottager." In page 359, he observes, that the insular chieftains have quitted the castles that sheltered their ancestors, and generally live near them, in mansions not very spacious or splendid: " Yet," says he, " they (the modern houses) bear testimony to the progress of arts and civility, as they shew that rapine and surprise are no longer dreaded."

Can there be a greater variance than between these two passages and what our author insinuates in regard to the neighbouring clans? Or can any thing be more clearly

clearly demonstrative of Dr. *Johnson*'s partial, vague, and contradictory mode of writing?

" There is neither shame from ignorance, nor pride from knowledge."—Unless the Doctor has a mind to retract what he formerly allowed in favour of the clergy, gentry, and middle rank of people, this observation can only regard the lowest class of the inhabitants; and we have already seen with how little reason or justice they can become the objects of such critical animadversion. It is not their natural character to be thought ignorant of such things as commonly belong to their state and situation in life; and few, I believe, of the same rank in other countries, extend their knowledge much beyond those bounds.

Had the Doctor and they been able to converse freely in the same language, he would

would have discovered in them a degree of acuteness, sagacity, and intelligence, not very common perhaps in the same station of life; and which, I am persuaded, he would have had no great inclination to relate. That much, with a knowledge of their own domestic operations and concerns, is all that could be expected from them; and it ought to have exempted them from so scurrilous an attack. A comprehensive view of the present state of the country, or a minute acquaintance with the history of former times, was not to be obtained in huts and cottages. Their ignorance of such matters must necessarily be great, and their knowledge but little. There can, therefore, be no reason for *shame* from the one, nor for *pride* from the other.

" Neither curiosity to inquire, nor vanity to communicate."—In different parts of his work, he gives a very different account of their curiosity. In particular, in page 116, he represents them as much addicted to curiosity, a love of talk, and a fondness for new topics of conversation. But the Doctor has a peculiar knack at *making* them what he pleases, and *unmaking* them again, as different purposes may require.

If they have really so little desire to communicate, as is here asserted, I should be glad to know how he came by those numerous anecdotes in his Journey to the *Hebrides*, relating to the ancient friendships, feuds, intermarriages, military alliances, and other transactions, of many of the insular chiefs. He often insists that we have no written vouchers for these things, nor any other authority than what is founded on tradition alone. If this be true, I can see no other channel through which he could have received his intelligence, than by *communication* from the inhabitants.

Either

Either then, contrary to what the Doctor has asserted elsewhere, there must be records to furnish such materials; or, contrary to what he asserts in this place, the people must have had some little *vanity*, or desire, at least, *to communicate*. I maintain the affirmative of both; but both cannot be as the Doctor says, unless, indeed, we can suppose him to have obtained a retrospective view of things, by means of his *favourite* faculty of the *second sight*.

Besides this general argument, which I think is conclusive, the Doctor himself furnishes a variety of instances to prove a communicative disposition in the Highlanders. Of these I shall select only a few.

The old woman whose hut he entered, by the side of *Loch Ness*, seems to have been sufficiently communicative; for he tells us, page 67, " that she was willing enough

enough to display her whole system of economy." This much, surely, is all the information that could be expected from her. The Doctor, in his turn, seems as willing to describe as she was willing to display; and it must be confessed that he has acquitted himself in that part with great dexterity. The minuteness of trifling detail and the garrulity peculiar to an old woman are so happily hit off, that one would think it *natural* for our traveller to exhibit that character. Were such a representation wanted in a scenic entertainment, Dr. *Johnson* promises fair to give general satisfaction.—His landlord at *Anoch*, likewise, seems to have had no great aversion to a pretty free communication; and the Doctor acknowledges his being indebted to him for many particulars, which he was desirous to know, relating to that part of the country.—But the most direct instance against the Doctor's assertion

assertion we have in page 251. He there tells us, that their desire of information was keen, their inquiry frequent, and that every body was communicative.

Enough, I presume, has been said upon these heads for the conviction of the reader, and too much, perhaps, for his patience; but as the attack was complicated, it was necessary the defence against each part should be particular.

In the above passage, the whole artillery of Dr. *Johnson*'s malice is brought to the field at once. Before, he generally levelled but one engine at a time; namely, either the pride, the poverty, or the ignorance of the country. But here he plays them off all together; and that they might not fail of the intended execution, he has taken care to succour them with a fresh recruit of calumny.

As usual, he asserts with a boldness that bids defiance to contradiction; but an insolent and peremptory manner, the pomp of an inflated diction, and the *gingle* of a quaint and laboured antithesis, are left to supply the place of argument and proof. By such a parade, no doubt, he hoped to do much; but we have seen how little he has been able to effect. The weapons which he aimed with so much care have been flung in vain. His own testimony has blunted the point of every shaft.

We can therefore only say, that if Dr. *Johnson*'s praises be well founded, his censures must be destitute of truth. It is impossible we can give our assent to contraries at one and the same time. But whichever we may chuse to believe, our author stands in that mortifying kind of predicament, that he can be trusted no further than he agrees with other writers.

This

This description in *caricature*, which the Doctor gives of the Islanders in general, seems so much the more inexplicable, that he speaks favourably of every individual whom he had occasion to know or converse with.

The behaviour even of the lower class of people, on every occasion, seemed to please him. The two *horse-hirers*, who attended him from *Inverness* to the ferry-passage for *Sky*, acquitted themselves so much to his satisfaction, for their fidelity, care, and alertness, that he recommends them at parting to any future travellers. When travelling from place to place, in the different islands which he visited, the men who were occasionally employed either as guides, or to walk by his horse through rough grounds, have all obtained their share of his praise, for their care, attention, and civil behaviour. The rowers of boats, or mariners of vessels, in passing from one ifland to another, he allows to be dexterous and obliging. Every hut he enters gives him ftriking fpecimens of hofpitality, and the kind and liberal difpofition of the inhabitants. Wherever there is a houfe, he fays, the traveller finds a welcome. And, in fhort, it was the good behaviour of the lower clafs of people that drew from him that remarkable obfervation in page 60, " that civility feems part of the national character of Highlanders."

As to the better fort, again, he may be faid to be even lavifh of praife. His *encomiums* are as frequent as there were families he vifited, or perfons he converfed with. A few inftances of this kind will be fufficient.

At the laird of *Mackinnon*'s in Sky, the company was numerous and genteel, and fo very agreeable to the Doctor, that their converfation fufficiently compenfated the

interruption

interruption given to his journey by the badness of the weather. At *Raasay*, he was enchanted by every species of elegance. At *Dunvegan*, the seat of the laird of *Macleod*, he had tasted *lotus*, and was in danger of forgetting that he was ever to depart. The amiable manners, and many other virtues, of the young laird of *Col*, are frequently and liberally displayed. At Dr. *Maclean*'s, a physician in Mull, he found very kind and good entertainment, and very pleasing conversation. At *Inch Kenneth*, the residence of Sir *Allan* Maclean, he says he could have been easily persuaded to a longer stay; but life could not be always passed in delight. And, of Mr. *Maclean*, a minister in *Mull*, at whose house he staid a night, our traveller says, that the elegance of his conversation, and strength of judgment, would make him conspicuous in places of greater celebrity.

After

After hearing Dr. *Johnson* give such testimonies as these, in favour of the Highlanders, could any one believe, that in the passage I have last quoted from his work, he was speaking of the same people? *Individually*, he allows them to be entitled to commendation; but *collectively*, he loads them with slander and abuse. Though every man is *civil*, the whole taken together make a nation of *savages* and *barbarians*. Though he saw *plenty* and elegance every where, the country is pining in *poverty*, and destitute of every comfort of life. And though he gives so many instances of an uncommon share of *learning* and *knowledge* being pretty widely diffused among them, he pronounces them, in the bulk, to be an *illiterate* and *ignorant* people.

This surely is a very extraordinary way of drawing conclusions. To prove its absurdity, would be to prove a self-evident proposition.

proposition. As well might Dr. *Johnson* pretend to tell us, that if a number of pieces of pure gold were to be fused together in a furnace, the product wou'd turn out a mass or aggregate of a baser metal.

Page 257, he observes, that in the houses of the chiefs were preserved what accounts remained of past ages. " But the chiefs," says he, " were sometimes ignorant and careless, and sometimes kept busy by turbulence and contention; and one generation of ignorance effaces the whole series of unwritten history. Books are faithful repositories, which may be a while neglected or forgotten; but when they are opened again, will again impart their instruction: memory once interrupted, is not to be recalled. Written learning is a fixed luminary, which, after the cloud that had hidden has passed away, is again bright in its proper station. Tradition is but a meteor,

meteor, which, if once it falls, cannot be rekindled."

Here the Doctor is making his approaches very fast, and is now almost on the point of springing the mine which he has been so long in digging. In this place he prepares his reader, by an artful insinuation, for what he means to assert boldly afterwards. To invalidate the credit of Highland antiquities, seems to have been the great object of his journey. As the Doctor hates the trouble of much inquiry, and to accomplish this end in the most easy and compendious manner, he finds it necessary first to suppose that we had no written accounts of past ages, and then, but without any proof, to convert that supposition into a matter of fact.

I am as ready as Dr. *Johnson* to acknowledge the superiority of books over *mere* tradition, when they are written with candour

candour and care. But even books themselves are not always to be trusted. There are false books as well as false traditions; and the *Journey* to the *Hebrides*, I am afraid, is one of those books which will not be thought to deserve the name of a *faithful repository*. As to the circumstance of our writings, I shall speak to that point in its place; and doubt not but the *good* Doctor will appear to as much disadvantage in that part of his story, as he has already done in many other cases.

Let us suppose, however, in the mean time, were it only for argument's sake, that, some centuries ago, there were few or no written authorities among us; what would be the consequence? Not surely that general one which Dr. *Johnson* so unlogically affirms, namely, " That one generation of ignorance effaces the whole series of unwritten history." One or more chiefs, at a particular time, might, as he says, be careless,

careless, not very knowing, or kept busy by turbulence and contention; but I see no reason to conclude from thence, that the whole of the chiefs, and all the generation of men then living, should be so too. Unless, therefore, contrary to all probability, we are to suppose this much, our traveller's inference cannot follow, and his argument amounts to nothing. For, if there could not be a whole generation of ignorance at once, the whole series of unwritten history could not be effaced.

At the same time, I am not inclined to lay more stress upon mere vague tradition than other men. I am certain I would trust it as little as the *scrupulous* Doctor himself, and perhaps even a little less than he would, when it might seem to lean to a favourable purpose. In defending the vulgar doctrine of the *second sight*, he had no better foundation to rest upon; and yet he finds no difficulty in telling us upon that head,

head, that when we are unable to decide by other reasons, we must be content to yield to the force of such testimony.

Tradition, however, in the liberal sense of the word, has, in all ages, been deemed of some weight; and the best writers have often appealed to it, not only when other evidence has been wanting, but likewise as an auxiliary proof. The tradition regarded by the Highlanders, in matters of any consequence, was of that nature which could not easily deceive them. It was so closely interwoven with the custom and constitution of the country, that it could not be separated from them; and it was handed down from one generation to another, not by *Bards* and *Seannachies* only, but by the general voice and consent of a whole nation.

It was not of that vague and uncertain nature which Dr. *Johnson* represents it to be;

be; nor of that weak and unmanly kind, which he himself has admitted, on particular occasions, as sufficient. But one thing is perfectly evident, that when tradition is for the country, the Doctor rejects it; and when it operates on the other side, he admits it as proof. Such a partial mode of representation speaks for itself.

That the Highlanders were not so liable to be imposed upon by the flattering compositions and tales of their *Bards* and *Seannachies*, as our traveller would insinuate, is beyond all dispute. Besides those who were employed in those professions, there were multitudes in the country who spent most of their leisure hours in hearing, recording, and rehearsing the atchievements of their ancestors and countrymen. Among these, there were many who composed poems in a strain equal to the *Bards* themselves; and such private persons were always a check upon the *Bards* and *Seannachies*

nachies by profession, to prevent their deviating from the truth.

Though the *Bards* and *Seannachies* are no longer retained as formerly, this custom in the country is not yet discontinued. I myself, as well as thousands still alive, have seen and heard instances of what I have just now mentioned. Had the Doctor chosen it, he might likewise have been a witness to such recitals, notwithstanding the cursory view he took of the country. He acknowledges, however, that he had seen some who remembered the practice. This much from him is pretty well; though, by putting the matter a little further back, it shews a visible design to *narrow* the real truth.

But though the Doctor's curiosity did not lead him this far, he might very easily, had he been a little more inquisitive, have heard much more concerning this matter than

than he has thought fit to communicate. It is not to be supposed that the Highlanders would have concealed any thing of what they knew, though he sometimes insinuates as much, had he but known how to make his inquiries agreeable.

But the misfortune was, that the Doctor was commonly deficient in that respect. His first question was generally rude, and the second a downright insult. This surely was not the most likely way to encourage intelligence. Yet there is still more reason to believe, from the general tenor of his work, either that he chose to avoid knowing what might be in favour of the country, or to misrepresent or suppress it when known, than that he should be refused information, had he been capable of asking it like a gentleman.

No other traveller but himself has attempted to tax the inhabitants of this country with a difpofition to conceal the truth. I could cite feveral inftances from his own tour to prove the contrary. In particular, the ftories which he relates of the kirk of Culloden, and of the cave in the ifland of *Egg*, are manifeftly againft the country. Is it credible, therefore, that they fhould be lefs ready to communicate faithfully what might be in its favour? But as the Doctor gives thefe, and fuch like anecdotes, without the leaft expreffion of diffidence, it would feem that he never believed he was told the truth, but when he was told fomething to the prejudice of Scotland.

Page 258. It feems to be univerfally fuppofed, fays he, that much of the local hiftory was preferved by the *Bards*, of whom one is faid to have been retained by every great family. He then tells us, that he made feveral inquiries after thefe Bards, and received fuch anfwers as, for a while, made him pleased with his increase of knowledge; but, alas! he adds immediately after, that he was only pleased, " as he had not then learned how to estimate the narration of a Highlander."

This *sage* remark at the end of his paragraph is owing to the same *important* cause, as a similar observation formerly about the business of *brogue-making*; namely, some inconsiderable variation in the subsequent accounts he received. At one time he was told that a great family had a *Bard* and a *Seannachie*, who were the poet and historian of the house; and an old gentleman said, that he remembered one of each. But unluckily, another conversation informed him, that the same man was both *Bard* and *Seannachie*; and this variation discouraged the *accurate* and *consistent* Dr. *Johnson*.

It is the more surprising to hear him express any discouragement in this case, that he immediately after gives so easy and natural a solution of the difficulty himself, if it may be thought deserving of that name. He says very properly, as he said before concerning the two different accounts of *brogue-making*, that the practice might be different in different times, or at the same time in different families. This most certainly was the true state of the matter; and this plain account of it removes the stumbling-block at once.

I will venture to assert, from my own personal knowledge of some people, from whom the Doctor received a great part of his intelligence, that the affair was explained to him in this very manner upon the spot. I will still go further; I have authority to say so. It is, therefore, worse than childish in our author to continue still to express his distrust, on account of a circumstance so clearly reconcileable both to reason and truth, and for which he himself has furnished a solid and satisfactory explanation.

To discover doubts in such plain cases, is a mark of weakness; but to lay hold of them as a handle for general calumny, if a man is not a downright ideot, is wicked to the last degree. Such trivial variations are not only common, but even unavoidable, in the discourse of different persons, all the world over; and if that could be reckoned a valid objection, we find likewise from experience, that the writings of the most approved authors are liable to the same condemnation.

We have often seen our traveller driven to pitiful shifts to criminate the country; but, like many others, the present one happily proves only his own rancour and disingenuity, not the insincerity of Scotch or Highland narration.

But

But to follow out this matter a little further, as the Doctor builds so much upon it afterwards, let me seriously ask him, if he really found so much improbability in the above narrations, as to make him the complete infidel he pretends? If he did, he is truly a man "*of little faith*;" of much less, indeed, than I should have expected from the conjurer of the *Cock-lane* ghost, or the champion of the *second sight*.

Was the Doctor weak enough to believe, that the world would deem it a sufficient argument to overturn any fact, that one part of its history was related by one person, and another part by another? Yet, by his own confession, this is clearly the case in the present point in dispute. In *England*, I presume, and in every other country whatever, a man might receive, from different people, different parts of information concerning the same thing. That, however,

however, could be no juſt ground for charging the inhabitants with impoſition.

In ſuch a caſe, I believe, the Doctor would be ready enough to acquit the *Engliſh*, and perhaps any other nation but the Scotch. If this be ſo, it only proves, that he was ſo ridiculouſly extravagant as to expect more from the Highlanders than from any other people. But how could he imagine that every man he met with, even the moſt illiterate in other reſpects, ſhould be a complete maſter of the whole hiſtory and antiquities of his country? None but a ſnarling *Cynic* would find fault with a deficiency of this kind; and no man of a moderate degree of experience in common life would expect ſuch abſolute preciſion, even from the moſt knowing of the better ſort themſelves.

But let me interrogate my *good* friend the Doctor a little further. Did he never read

read in one historian any particular that was omitted by another? Did he ever read any two historians who were exactly the same? and, if they were exactly the same in all points, would he call their works different histories? Does he think it impossible, that any two writers, having each the strictest regard to truth, should disagree in some points of narration relating to the same fact? and, if they should so disagree, does he think *that* would be a sufficient cause for rejecting their authority, and impeaching their veracity, in all other cases whatever?

If the Doctor answers these queries in a manner that is consistent with the common sense of mankind, he must drop his objections to the accounts which he received of the *brogue-makers* and *Seannachies*; unless he intends to maintain, that *tradition* ought to be more certain and infallible than his " faithful repository" of *written history.*

If

If any thing more should be wanting to convince Dr. *Johnson* of the inconclusiveness of his reasoning, let me entreat his leave to state a similar case; for, as the *Bards* and *Seannachies* were of the domestic order of people, I shall confine myself to that line.

Let us suppose, then, that a traveller in England is told, that, in one house, there is both a *cook-maid* and a *chamber-maid*, but that, in another house, the same person acted in these two different capacities. This is exactly a parallel instance with that under consideration; and none will doubt, I presume, but there are many examples of both kinds on the south-side of the Tweed. Where then would be the inconsistency in these different accounts? Or would it be reasonable to infer, from such a difference in the economy of different families, either that the intelligence must be false, or that the existence of such

female

female occupations was rendered doubtful? And yet one or other of thefe muſt follow, if the Doctor's concluſions concerning the *Bards* and *Scannachies* are allowed to be juſt.

I could have illuſtrated this ſubject from the various profeſſions of the *parti-coloured* gentry; but I choſe to exemplify in the female line, as the Doctor, I am told, is more than commonly attached to the ſex, for a man of his advanced years. I ſhall leave him, therefore, to ſettle the matter with *Kate* and *Moll*, as well as he is able; and doubt not, but the " priſtine reminiſcence of juvenile jucundity" will induce him, for their fakes at leaſt, to renounce an argument which would infallibly deprive the poor wenches of their places. Should he provoke them by his obſtinacy, I am in ſome pain for the conſequences. The Doctor's " mode of ratiocination," I am afraid, could not long hold out againſt the

the more *simple* but *weighty* arguments of the *spit* and *mop-staff*.

There appears nothing in the accounts concerning the *Bards* and *Seannachies*, which so much *discouraged* the Doctor, that can either call in question the belief of their own existence, or throw the least doubt on the histories of the families in which they resided. In most great houses there was one of each; while, in some others, there was a Bard only. In the latter case, however, the accuracy of the family history could be but little affected; as the Bard, whose business it was to repeat the genealogies of the chiefs, and to sing the atchievements of their ancestors, must be no inconsiderable Seannachie, or antiquarian, in order to be qualified for those purposes.

The *Bards* and *Seannachies* were not only "supposed," as Dr. *Johnson* expresses himself,

self, " to preserve the local history," but they actually did preserve it; and they were not only " said to have been retained by every great family," but they really were retained. The truth of this does not rest upon tradition alone. The charters of many great families bear witness concerning them; and they are likewise mentioned by many eminent writers. Both these, as being written authority, must almost persuade the unbelieving Doctor himself to renounce his infidelity.

Mr. *Innes*, who, in general, is no great friend to the Bards, tells us, that in the thirteenth century, at the coronation of *Alexander* III., a Highland *Bard* pronounced an oration on the genealogy of the kings of Scotland. As this happened in the year 1249, before the destruction of so many of our records by Edward I. of England, and in the presence of the three estates of the kingdom,

kingdom, assembled on that occasion, we may naturally suppose the Bards and Seannachies of those times to have been pretty accurate in their accounts; otherwise, it must have been difficult to find one who would venture to undertake such a task. At so public a solemnity there must have been many present who could have contradicted him, if he erred in his narration; and amidst the multitude of written testimonies then existing, he was sure of being detected, supposing none of his auditors had been able to correct him.

The same author allows, in page 237, that this genealogy was one of the most accurate performances of the kind which had ever existed.

The same circumstance is mentioned by all *Fordun*'s continuators, and likewise by *Major*.

Ammianus

Ammianus Marcellinus, book xv. page 51, says, "The Bards sung the remarkable atchievements of their heroes, in verse, to the sweet melody of their harps."

Valesius, who pretends to write notes on this author, betrays a gross ignorance of his meaning, as well as of the profession or employment of the Bards, when he says, in page 93, " that the Bards were a species of parasites or buffoons, who diverted the soldiers at their banquets with their jests and mimical gestures." This is a most false and ridiculous account of the matter, and entirely explains away the meaning of his author; for *Ammianus Marcellinus* says no such thing. Besides, it is well known that they had others who acted in the capacity he mentions; that is, *jesters*, who likewise constituted a part of their domestics, as well as the Bards.

In page 258, the Doctor says, " that an old gentleman told him, that he remembered one of each," namely, a *Bard* and a *Seannachie*. There was no occasion to make the gentleman very old to remember this much, as will soon be made appear. But Dr. *Johnson* does not chuse to stop here; for, in the very next page, he sets every evidence for the existence of either *Bards* or *Seannachies*, beyond all memory whatever. His words are, " I was told by a gentleman, who is generally acknowledged the greatest master of *Hebridian* antiquities, that there had been once both Bards and Senachies; and that *Senachi* signified *the man of talk*, or of conversation; but that neither Bard nor Senachi had existed for some centuries."

Here the testimony of the old gentleman, who said that he had seen both a Bard and a Seannachie, is entirely set aside,

aside, by the contrary testimony of another gentleman, who, as Dr. *Johnson* says, told him, that none of either had existed for some centuries. I am rather apt to suspect the accuracy of the Doctor's representation, concerning this latter gentleman. Almost every man in the Highlands knows the contrary to be true; and if any one told him what he asserts, we may doubt his title to the character of an antiquarian. But the Doctor, with his usual caution, conceals his author's name; which certainly was prudent, as by this means the hazard of a personal refutation is avoided.

It was well judged in the Doctor, however, to make his *gentleman* so great a master of *Hebridian* antiquities. By this policy he secures a better title to be believed; and immediately after, he makes his own use of what he pretends to have received from such *undoubted* authority. " Whenever the practice of recitation was difused,"

difused," says he, " the works, whether poetical or historical, perished with the authors; for in those times nothing had been written in the *Earse* language."

There has been occasion to observe, oftener than once, that it was the great object of the Doctor's *Journey*, to find out some pretence or other for denying the authenticity of the ancient compositions in the *Gaelic* language; and now that design begins to unfold itself beyond a possibility of doubt. To effect his purpose, he takes a short but very ingenious method. He finds it only necessary to say, that no Bards have existed for some centuries; that, as nothing was then written in the *Gaelic* language, their works must have perished with themselves; and consequently, that every thing now attributed to them, by their modern countrymen, must be false and spurious.

As

As the Doctor gives no authority for the facts, from which he draws this inference, he might as well have remained at home, as he says upon another occasion, and have fancied to himself all that he pretends to have heard on this subject. His bare word, without leaving *Fleet-street*, would have been just as good as his bare word after returning from the *Hebrides*. A *Journey*, however, was undertaken; though there is every reason to believe, that it was not so much with a view to obtain information, as to give a degree of sanction to what he had before resolved to assert.

But though there had really been no Bards or Seannachies for such a length of time, and though the *Gaelic* had really been an unwritten language, there is no reason for supposing that all the ancient compositions perished immediately with their authors. I have already shewn, that the practice of recitation was not formerly confined to the Bards and Seannachies alone, and that it is not altogether difused even in our own times. It muft therefore follow, that many of their works would ftill be preferved by this means only, even after the Bards and Seannachies, by profeffion, might ceafe to exift.

There is no neceffity, however, for trufting to this argument alone. I may hereafter take an opportunity of fhewing, that the *Gaelic* has not always been an uncultivated language; which will weaken one part of the foundation on which the Doctor builds. In the mean time, I fhall produce fome facts to evince, that the domeftic offices in queftion exifted much later than he is willing to allow; and that, I prefume, will go nigh to fap the remaining part of his fabric.

It is not neceffary, nor will I pretend exactly to fay, when the office of *Seannachie*, as diftinct distinct from that of *Bard*, fell into disuse. By this I mean only the Seannachie by profession; for as to Seannachies from choice, and for the amusement of themselves and friends, they have always existed; and there are several, and those not contemptible ones, both of the better and lower sort of people, still living in the country. It will be enough to shew, from well known facts, that the regular profession of Bard, who occasionally likewise officiated as Seannachie, has not been so long out of fashion.

The *Macewens* had free lands in *Lorn* in Argyleshire, for acting as Bards to the family of *Argyle*, to that of *Breadalbane*, and likewise to Sir *John Macdougal* of Dunolly, in 1572. The two last of the race were *Airne* and his son *Neil*.

I have now before me an Elegy upon the Death of Sir *Duncan Dow Campbel* of Glenurchy,

Glenurchy, composed by *Neil Macewen*. The date, which is 1630, is in the body of the poem. How long he lived after this, I cannot take upon me to say; but as there is much of the history and genealogy of the family interwoven with the performance, he must certainly have been both *Bard* and *Seannachie*.

John Macodrum in North Uist, who is still alive, and not a very old man, had a yearly allowance from the late Sir *James Macdonald* of Slate, which, I believe, may be still continued, by the present Lord *Macdonald*. I have, in my possession, many of his compositions, which are far from being destitute of merit.

I have likewise, in my hands, some poems, composed by one Bard *Mathonach*; in one of which he acknowledges to have received gold from the earl of *Seaforth*, at parting on board the ship that was to carry his

his benefactor out of the kingdom, after the battle of Sheriffmuir, in the year 1715. Another of his poems is in praise of the late Lord *Lovat*, who made him a present of a gun. Whether he was retained in the official quality of *Bard*, by either of those noblemen, I cannot pretend to determine.

Many of my readers know, that one of the most remarkable *Bards* of modern times, was *John Macdonald*, descended of the family of *Keppoch* in Lochaber. He was commonly called *John Lom*; and sometimes *John Mantach* or *Mabach*, from an impediment in his speech. He composed as many poems as would fill a pretty large volume. A great number of them are still extant, and many of them are in my possession. Most of his compositions have great merit.

He lived from the reign of *Charles* I. to the time of king *William*. But what may startle

startle Dr. *Johnson* not a little, *Charles* II. settled a yearly pension upon him, for officiating as his Bard. As many of his poems mention the chief transactions of the times, as well as the names of the princes, chiefs, and nobility, whose atchievements he sung, they carry their dates in their bosoms, and fix the æra in which they were composed. He lived to an extreme old age, so that there are still a few people of very advanced years who remember to have seen him.

But to come more closely to the point. I wish the Doctor may preserve his temper and patience when I inform him, that *Neil Macvurich*, descended of the famous race of *Macvurichs*, Bards and Seannachies to the *Clanronald* family, is still alive, and enjoys free lands from *Allan Macdonald* of Clanronald, as his Bard and Seannachie. This man writes the *Celtic* or *Gaelic* character, which was taught him

by

by his predeceffors, but he underſtands no other language or character whatever.

This piece of intelligence muſt equally furpriſe and gall our traveller; but, as the thing is true, there is no help for it. There is no fact whatever more certain or better known; and it could be atteſted by the moſt reputable people in that part of the kingdom, if the evidence of " Highland narration," which the Doctor has fo often reprobated, could be admitted as fatiſ= factory. But what is ſtill more, he might eaſily, while in the country, have had the laſt and beſt proof of what is here aſſerted, even ocular demonſtration. He might have feen the Bard *Macvurich*, and others, with his own eyes; and he might likewife have had the fame unerring teſtimony for the exiſtence of many manuſcripts in the *Gaelic* language, for feveral centuries back.

This mode of information, however, the Doctor always avoided. It would not have answered the purpose with which he had set out. His plan was laid; and he never wished to see or hear any thing that could induce him to alter it. As, therefore, he was determined to write in the very manner he has done, he has this *one* claim to virtue at least, that he did not chuse to write against conviction.

These instances are but a few of many that might be given; but, I flatter myself, they will prove sufficient to satisfy the public, if not even Dr. *Johnson* himself, that his *Hebridian* antiquarian, if such there was, has grosly misinformed him; and consequently, that the ingenious *syllogism*, which he has formed upon that information, however agreeable to *mode* and *figure*, is not agreeable to *truth*.

Unless

Unless the Doctor would have every testimony rejected but his own, I hope I have given reasons for believing, that there have been always regular *Bards* and *Seannachies* in the country, and that there are still some of both; that the practice of *recitation* has not yet ceased, and that the *Gaelic* has not been an unwritten language; and, of course, that the Doctor's conclusion, from the opposite *premises*, does not necessarily follow, namely, " That the works of the ancient Bards and Seannachies, whether poetical or historical, perished with the authors."

In addition to what has been said, I can assure the reader, that many poems of the Bards I have already mentioned, as well as of several others, are in my own possession; and that many other gentlemen, in different parts of the Highlands, have likewise large collections, among which there are productions of very old dates. These are

are always open to the infpection of curiofity, when a ftranger fignifies a defire to fee them; <u>and a confiderable number of them have been lately publifhed</u>, in a moderate volume, for the fatisfaction of fuch as may not have an opportunity of vifiting the country, and feeing the originals.

In regard to our hiftorical works of any long ftanding, I have already mentioned, that they fuffered greatly by the ravages of *Edward* the Firft, and of *Cromwell*. The Doctor ftill continues to reproach us with the want of them, though he knows by what means there is fuch a deficiency in our national annals; and that the unhappy divifions among ourfelves, at thofe two periods, gave an eafy opportunity to thofe inveterate enemies to the antiquities of *Scotland*, to deftroy fome part of our records, and carry off another.

As it now appears, that many of our Seannachies were also *Bards*, it may naturally be supposed, that much of our ancient history was in verse. The same practice obtained in all other nations, in the early ages, and in the like circumstances. Accordingly, many of our poems consist of descriptions of battles, deaths of heroes, and concise narratives of other historical facts.

Page 260, he says, " Whether the man of talk was a historian, whose office was to tell truth, or a story-teller, like those which were in the last century, and perhaps are now among the *Irish*, whose trade was only to amuse, it now would be vain to inquire." It would be far from *vain* to make this *inquiry*, were it necessary; but the matter has been already cleared up. The case is sufficiently plain; but the Doctor generally creates doubts where

there

there are none, and puzzles his reader with difficulties of his own making.

In the fame page, he proceeds, "Probably the laureat of a clan was always the fon of the laſt laureat. The hiſtory of the race could no otherwife be communicated, or retained; but what genius could be expected in a poet by inheritance?" Though the Doctor ſpeaks doubtfully of this fact, he concludes with a triumphant *query*, in the fame confident manner as if he had proved it.

I ſhall grant him, indeed, that genius, any more than other endowments, cannot be expected to go by inheritance; and I ſhould as little think it neceſſary for the fon of the laſt laureat, as he *wittily* calls the Highland Bard, to be a poet, as for the fon of our *pompous* journaliſt to be a *pedant*. Sons may often poſſefs qualities very oppoſite to thofe of their fathers. A mere blockhead

blockhead has sometimes, no doubt, been the son of a very good Bard; and there can be no reason why the offspring of even a Dr. *Johnson,* though without a title by inheritance, should not hereafter be distinguished for truth, candour, good breeding, and other virtues.

If the son of the last Bard had a genius equal to the office, there is no doubt, but among a friendly and generous people, it would be reckoned an act of justice to prefer him to another; but if he was found deficient in that respect, it is evident, from the practice of the country, that he could not succeed. There were regular schools for the education of Bards, called, in the Gaelic language, *Scoil Bhairdeachd,* in which the youth, or candidates for the profession, underwent a long course of discipline; and, after all this preparation, such as were found incapable were always rejected. From this it would seem, that

those

those who had the superintendency of those schools paid a strict regard to the judicious rule of the ancients—*nascimur poetæ*. But more of this hereafter.

In the same page he still goes on. "The nation was wholly illiterate. Neither Bards nor Seannachies could write or read." I wish the Doctor had fixed the period to which he alludes; but that, like all other points accompanied with a charge, he prudently leaves undetermined. But let him choose what time he pleases, it will be easy to shew the fallacy and unprincipled presumption of these assertions.

The early introduction of learning into Scotland is acknowledged by all the histories of Europe. In the first ages of Christianity, for our traveller, I suppose, does not carry his observations back to the times of the *Druids*, our learning, no doubt, was chiefly confined to the priesthood. But what then?

then? Will the Doctor pretend to say, that the case was then different in any other country? If he will not, I should be glad to know wherein the force of his first assertion consists. While we had priests only, the nation could not be " wholly illiterate" at any period of time.

Many instances have been already mentioned to prove the progress of literature among us, before the universal gloom of *Gothic* desolation; and the Doctor himself acknowledges, in page 56, that soon after its revival it found its way to *Scotland*. Where then will he fix the period for justifying his present assertion? If there is truth in history, if there is truth in Dr. *Johnson* himself, what he now says must appear to be unjust; and that the Scotch nation was not *illiterate* at any time, or in any sense of the word, while other nations could pretend to have been more enlightened.

Being thus driven from his poſt, our author has no refuge but in ignorance or wilful miſrepreſentation. To a man of the leaſt dignity of mind, or ſenſe of honour, either muſt be intolerable. But let him take which ſtation he pleaſes, he will find himſelf diſappointed in both. He forfeits every pretenſion to wiſdom or to virtue; whether he prefers the weak ſhelter of the fool, or the more obſtinate retreat of the knave.

It is always with reluctance I have recourſe to any aſperity of language; but the inſolence and injuſtice of Dr. *Johnſon* demand ſome ſeverity. When a man dares to traduce a nation with ſo much indecent freedom, it would be *falſe delicacy*, indeed, not to treat him, in his turn, with all that contempt that is conſiſtent with truth. Oppoſed to a whole people, an individual ſinks into nothing; and, if he forgets the ſuperior reſpect that is due to the many, he neceſſarily

neceſſarily diveſts himſelf of all title to complaiſance.

As to his next aſſertion, that " neither Bards nor Seannachies could write or read," I would aſk him what he means? If it is that the ancient Bards and Seannachies could not write or read *Engliſh*, I will not diſpute the point. That language was as foreign to the old *Celtic* or *Scotch* Bards and Seannachies, as it is to the *French* or *Italian* poets and hiſtorians at this day. Will the Doctor call the latter ignorant, becauſe they neither write nor read the language of *his* country? If he will not, the abſurdity of his inſinuation againſt the former is too evident to require an anſwer on that account.

But as he told us before, and repeats it afterwards, that nothing had been written formerly in what he calls the *Earſe*, his meaning more probably is, that our Bards and Seannachies could neither write nor read

read any language whatever. If this really be so, the answer is short and easy, and I will tell him, without any ceremony, that the allegation is false and untrue.

As to the Doctor's *Earse*, it has a filthy sound, and I must reject it, as never being a word of ours. It is only a barbarous term introduced by strangers, and seems to be a corruption of *Irish*. The Caledonians always called their native language *Gaelic*; and they never knew it by any other name.

If we go back to so early a period as the institution of the monasteries or abbacies of *I*, or *Iona*, *Oronsay*, and *Ardchattan*, &c. it is not to be doubted, but the use of letters was known in those seminaries, as well as in other places of the like kind in Europe. Were there no positive proofs of the fact now existing, it would be absurd to the last degree to deny it. Our monks must have understood the learned languages; and they must likewise have wrote them.

This

This much being granted, or rather self-evident, I can see no reason to prevent them from writing in their own language, more than the *religious* in all other countries. The *Gaelic* was the language in which they usually conversed; it was that into which it behoved the learned ones to be translated; and I well know it is the language by which my own lessons or exercises at school have been often explained to me, before I had acquired *English* enough to understand them otherwise. I shall proceed, however, to more positive proofs.

Of what has been written at *Iona*, I have heard, in particular, of a translation of St. Augustine *De Civitate Dei*, and a Treatise in *Physic*, which is very old. The former was in the possession of the late Mr. *Archibald Lambie*, minister of Killmartine in Argyleshire; and the latter was preserved in the Advocates library at *Edinburgh*, where, no doubt, it is still to be seen.

Two brothers of the name of *Bethune* were famous for the profession of physic, in the islands of *Islay* and *Mull*; and they were designed, from the places of their residence, * *Olla Ilich* and *Olla Mulich*. They were both educated in Spain, and were well versed in the Greek and Latin languages; but they did not understand one word of English.

Olla Ilich lived in the reign of *James* VI., and held free lands of his Majesty, as one of his physicians. He wrote a Treatise in Physic, in the Gaelic character, with quotations from *Hippocrates*. This manuscript was seen at Edinburgh some years ago, by a gentleman of my acquaint-

---

* *Olla* signifies a Doctor or Professor in any science, particularly in physic.

ance,

ance, in the poſſeſſion of Dr. *William Macfarlane*, now the laird of *Macfarlane*.

One Dr. *O'Connachar* of Lorn, in Argyleſhire, wrote all his preſcriptions in *Gaelic*; and his MS. has been ſeen by many gentlemen ſtill alive in that county.

There are, at preſent, two very old manuſcripts in the poſſeſſion of a gentleman in Argyleſhire. One of them contains the Adventures of *Smerbie More*, one of the predeceſſors of the family of Argyle; who, as appears from the genealogy of that family, lived in the fifth century. The Doctor, perhaps, will not be much pleaſed to hear, that the other contains the Hiſtory of *Clanuiſneachain*, or the ſons of *Uſnoch*, a fragment in *Fingal*.

The ſame gentleman is likewiſe poſſeſſed of * Proſnachadh Catha *Chlann Domhnuill*,

---

* A ſpeech to cheer up the Macdonalds, when beginning the battle.

at the battle of Harlaw in 1411, compoſed by *Lachlan More Macvurich*, the Bard. This performance is in exact alphabetical order, like the Doctor's *famous* Dictionary. It contains four epithets upon every letter of the alphabet, beginning with the firſt letter, and ending with the laſt. Every epithet upon the ſame letter begins with that letter; which proves to a demonſtration, that ſome of the Bards, at leaſt, were not unacquainted with letters in that age.

In the body of the genealogy of the *Macvurich Bards*, this piece is mentioned, as the production of the abovenamed *Lachlan More*. Since I began theſe Remarks, the poem has been publiſhed by Mr. *Macdonald* in his collection, where it may be ſeen by the curious.

So far were the *Bards* from neglecting learning, that, as I have already obſerved, they had poetical ſchools *(Scoil Bhair-deachd*

deachd) regularly established at *Inverness*, in *Sky*, and other places. In these they went through certain exercises, or pieces of trials, which were prescribed to them. Such as did not acquit themselves to the satisfaction of the proper judges, were rejected, as unqualified for the office; and this often happened, after many years study and preparation.

Their subject, or thesis, was often proposed to them without any previous warning*. It was generally a sentence, though, sometimes, but a single word; and, at other times, it was altogether unintelligible, like the Barbara, celarent, Darii, ferio, &c. in logic. Of this last sort was the subject which *James* VI. gave to some

* Bishop Leslie observes, page 54. that—illis (pueris) exempla illustrium virorum, ad quorum se imitationem fingerent, rythmi cujusdam et carminis concentu, ad voluptatem illustrata proponere.——

poets,

poets, as a trial of skill in their profession*.

I can assert from as good authority as Dr. *Johnson* can pretend to, that, during even the later periods, some of the *Macvurich* (or *Macpherson*) race of Bards kept an academy in *Sky*, where they taught the *Greek* and *Latin* languages, as well as the *Gaelic* art of poetry.

If any ingenuous sense yet remains with the Doctor, he must necessarily *feel sore* at this account of the *Scotch* Bards. Igno-

---

* SUBJECT.

Snamhaid an Lach is an Fhaoilin
Da chois chapail chaoilin chorr.

ANSWER.

'D fhearas Deoch a Laimh Ri Alba,
A Cup Airgid agus Oir;
An Aite nach do fhaoil mi fhetin.
'S da chois chapail chaoilin chorr †.

† The poet who performed best was to get one cup-full of wine from the king's own hand, and another cup-full of gold, as his reward.

miny and difappointment ftare him, at once, in the face. His impudent affertions are difproved, and his darling purpofe defeated. He muft therefore be doubly ftung, if he is capable of fhame from falfehood, or of chagrin for the failure of his project.

But this *forgery* of our traveller, in afferting that the *Bards* were fo very illiterate, feems the more extraordinary, as he acknowledges, that there were regular fchools or colleges in *Sky*, and other places, for the education of *pipers*. His admitting this fact gives additional ftrength to what has been advanced concerning the academies of the Bards; as it is not very likely, that a people, who were fo attentive to an inferior art, fhould neglect the cultivation of genius, for a more important profeffion.

It muft be confeffed, however, that the fchools of the Bards began to be confiderably

ably upon the decline, within these last two centuries. Whether their not meeting with the usual encouragement was owing to their presuming too much on their own importance, to the introduction of new customs, or to their profession not appearing so necessary after the revival of letters, it is not material to inquire: nor need we be more surprised, that the race of Bards is now almost extinct, than that we hear no longer of the Harpers, Scialachies (tale-tellers), and Jesters of former times, or that even the bagpipe itself is approaching to the eve of its last *groans.* Our great people, like those of other nations, have found out new modes of amusement and expence, which probably, in their turn, will soon give way to others.

Upon the decay of their own seminaries at home, the Bards went to *Irish* schools of the same kind; the consequence of which was, that they contracted much of

the

the Irish poetical style, and a fondness for talking the Irish dialect of the Celtic language.

Many of our own countrymen, who were ignorant of this fact, have mistaken some of the writings and compositions of those *Irish-bred* Bards, for real Irish. Among the performances of this kind now extant, there are several which we would not hesitate to conclude to be true Irish, if we had not the most convincing proofs to the contrary.

We have a striking instance of this in the Elegy on Sir Duncan Dow Campbel, which has been mentioned above, and was composed by the Bard *Macewen* in 1630. This poem is, in many places, altogether unintelligible to most Highlanders; though other productions of a much earlier date, as being composed in the *Albion* dialect of the Celtic, are perfectly understood. In particular,

particular, there is a MS. poem by *Macleane*'s Bard, in praise of *Colin* earl of Argyle, in 1529, a complete century before the Elegy, which is entirely free from the obscurities to be found in that performance. But *Macewen* was one of those Bards who resided some time in Ireland. His poem is in the *Gaelic* character, and in his own hand-writing; and it is still preserved, among the papers of the family of *Breadalbane*, at Taymouth.

Besides adopting much of the poetical language of Ireland, the Bards who went to that country for education wrote many things in imitation of Irish pieces. This has given occasion to that people to claim, as their own, various compositions, which were in reality the productions of *Scotch* Bards.

Though I flatter myself, by this time, that the arrogant assertions of Dr. *Johnson*
will

will appear sufficiently refuted, and consequently, that the conclusions he so confidently draws from them must fall harmless to the ground; yet I shall subjoin a few observations more, which seem to offer themselves properly in this place.

It will not be denied, I believe, that our religious societies must have been possessed of learning. That they were so in an eminent degree, appears from their being in so great request among other nations; for *that* of *Iona*, in particular, sent professors to Cologne, Luvaine, Paris, and other places. Is it therefore probable, that, while they were employed in instructing foreigners, their own countrymen alone should remain uninformed? Such a supposition is too violent for common sense.

As a proof that learning was much cultivated among us, all the abbots, priors, and

and monks, of those seminaries, were real Highlanders. The Doctor might have been satisfied of this, from observing the names of *Macphingon* (Mackinnon) and *Mackenzie*, on the tomb-stones of two of the abbots of *Iona*; and the name of *Macdougall*, prior of *Ardchattan*, upon his tomb-stone at that place.

The same observation will hold, with regard to our nunneries. In that of *Iona*, one of the abbesses is designed, upon her tomb, in the patronymic manner, according to the custom of the country. The inscription both in *Latin* and in *Gaelic* is,—Domina Anna Donaldi Terleti filia,—Ann Ni mhic Dhonuill mhic Thearlaich. In English, it means,—Ann the daughter of Donald the son of Charles.

At *Oronsay*, and other places, the case was exactly the same. If therefore our religious seminaries, which were not a few, were

were filled with natives of the country, the nation cannot in any juſtice be ſaid to have been illiterate; though, contrary to all probability, literature had been confined to thoſe ſocieties alone. We likewiſe find, that there were monumental inſcriptions, in the *Gaelic* language, in very early periods of time. I ſee no reaſon then, if the Highlanders could cut out their language upon marble or ſtone, why they might not be able to write it upon parchment or paper.

Among other things, I might add, that as many of our kings, with their whole courts, reſided often in the Highlands, it is to be preſumed, whatever was known any where elſe, muſt have been known there alſo.

Before the time of King *Malcolm Cean More*, as may be judged from his very name, no other language but the *Gaelic* was spoken in Scotland. It was in compliment to *Margaret*, the queen of that monarch, and the eldest sister of *Edgar*, that the *English* language was first introduced even at court. This happened in 1068-9; and, from that æra, we may date, at least in the southern parts of the kingdom, the gradual decline of the *Celtic*, once the delight of all the courts of Europe.

It continued long, after this, to maintain its ground in the Highlands; but even there, at last, it began to be neglected to such a degree, that, but for the uncommon beauties of its poetical compositions, it would scarcely have existed, except amongst the vulgar alone. But, of late years, the better taste of a few has directed the attention of others to its superior excellence; and now again it begins, as it were, to recover new life.

Nothing can more effectually illustrate the copiousness and energy of the Gaelic language than this, that several of the poems, which have been lately published, and are now so much admired by the learned, were the *extempore* effusions of some men, who were not otherwise very learned themselves. But if, as Dr. *Johnson* expresses himself, they were strangers to the "splendors of ornamental erudition," they were equally so to that constraint, which is occasioned by the unnatural fetters of modern criticism. Genius prevailed over art; and they have found the power to please, without any guide but nature.

To what has been already said on these heads, I shall now beg leave to add the authority of Bishop Leslie; which most people, I presume, will deem fully as good in this case, as that of our *intelligent* and *candid* traveller. In page 157, that learned prelate says, " that *Eugenius* VII., in the year 699, took care to have many learned men aſſembled together from all parts of his dominions, and to be ſupported at his expence, who were to record not only the tranſactions or exploits of the *Scots*, but likewiſe thoſe of all other nations."

It may appear from hence, that the *Seannachies*, or hiſtorians of thoſe early times, were not an illiterate ſet of men, who could neither write nor read. When they became afterwards ſo very ignorant as the Doctor ſays, is incumbent upon him to point out; and before he urges that ignorance as a reproach, if he really can make it appear, he ought likewiſe to prove, that their ſouthern neighbours, at leaſt, were more knowing at the ſame time.

I ſhall next borrow an argument from Dr. *Johnſon*'s Journey, to confute himſelf. Through the whole courſe of this work, his own contradictions have ſerved me in much

much stead; and I take this opportunity of acknowledging my obligations, as the present assistance is none of the least considerable.

What he says, in speaking of *Iona* in particular, seems very inconsistent with what he has so lately advanced concerning the total ignorance of the country. As the passage is remarkable, I shall transcribe it for the sake of those who may not be possessed of his book.

"We were now," says he, page 346, "treading that illustrious island, which was once the luminary of the *Caledonian* regions, whence savage clans and roving barbarians derived the benefits of knowledge, and the blessings of religion. To abstract the mind from all local emotion would be impossible, if it were endeavoured, and would be foolish, if it were possible. Whatever draws us from the power of our senses; whatever makes the past, the distant, or the future predominate over the present, advances us in the dignity of thinking beings. Far from me and from my friends be such frigid philosophy as may conduct us indifferent and unmoved over any ground which has been dignified by wisdom, bravery, or virtue! That man is little to be envied, whose patriotism would not gain force upon the plain of *Marathon*, or whose piety would not grow warmer among the ruins of *Iona*."

In these transports of a not unlaudable enthusiasm, the celebrity of *Iona*, as an ancient seat of learning, is very strongly impressed. That title to fame must, indeed, be allowed to be just, which could extort such glowing strokes of eulogy from the pen of Dr. *Johnson*; whose testimony, when favourable to *Scotland*, no one can have reason to suspect.

It

It will naturally occur to every reader, that inftitutions of this fort, and *Iona* was but one of many, cannot afford proofs of an ignorant, rude, or barbarous people. The Doctor, by way of eminence, calls this the *luminary* of the *Caledonian* regions; and to fhew that he does not dignify it with that appellation in vain, he fays it was a fource of knowledge and religion to the inhabitants of the country. It is true, he talks, as ufual, of *favage clans* and *roving barbarians*. But as this may be the effect of a habit, which he cannot eafily lay afide, and by which, perhaps, he means no great harm, I fhall take no further notice of it at prefent, than only to obferve, that fuch *rough* epithets do not feem to be very happily chofen for the difciples of his revered *Iona*; a feminary, which he extols fo much for its wifdom and virtue.

Without wrangling about words, therefore, it is enough for *my* purpofe, that he has

has allowed the Highlanders to have derived knowledge from *Iona*; and for his *own* purpose, I am afraid, that conceſſion will rather be a little too much. He will find it no eaſy matter to perſuade the public, that a nation can be " *wholly illiterate*" and *inſtructed in knowledge* at the ſame time. There is a manifeſt repugnance between theſe two; and they never can be reconciled, unleſs, contrary to the uſual interpretation of the word, it will appear, from the Doctor's Dictionary, that *knowledge* is but another term for *ignorance*.

This inconſiſtency in the Doctor's manner of writing, exceeds thoſe *marvellous* variations in the different accounts of *brogue-making*, which ſtaggered our conſcientious traveller ſo much, as to make him queſtion the veracity of " Highland narration." The reader will be able to judge, by this time, to which of the parties ſuch a *ſtigma* moſt properly belongs. Should
he

he think of transferring it to the Doctor, I am only afraid he may create some embarrassment to himself. Having already seen so many of his contradictions, he must find him so *branded* all over, that he will hardly know where to stamp a new mark of disgrace.

I know not what degree of force the Doctor's patriotism might gain upon the plain of *Marathon*; but if we are to judge of his piety from his regard to truth, it seems not to have grown remarkably *warm* among the ruins of *Iona*. According to his own decision, therefore, " he is a man little to be envied."

Having, as he thinks, though without other proof than his bare assertion, established the non-existence of literature among us, he proceeds to apply that negative doctrine to our genealogies.

Page 261, he says, "The recital of genealogies has never subsisted within time of memory, nor was much credit due to such rehearsers, who might obtrude fictitious pedigrees, either to please their masters, or to hide the deficiency of their own memories.—Where the chiefs of the Highlands have found the histories of their descent is difficult to tell; for no *Earse* genealogy was ever written."

What our author means by what he calls "*within time of memory*," I am at a loss to know. If he means the *memory of man*, in its enlarged sense, he evidently contradicts himself in the preceding part of the same paragraph, where he says, that such recitals were anciently made when the heir of the family came to manly age. If he means the *memory* of any man now living, that would be but a trifling consideration, had it not even been already proved that the practice still continues.

As to the rehearsers of genealogies obtruding fictitious pedigrees on their masters, the Highlanders in general were too attentive to that branch of their antiquities, and too well versed in what related to their own descent and connections in the country, to admit easily of such an imposition; though there had been no other means of preventing it, than by rehearsal only. But it will immediately appear, that they had other securities for accuracy in that point.

When the Doctor tells us that " no *Earse* genealogy was ever written," he ought to have told us likewise upon what authority he founds so peremptory an assertion. Contrary to a similar falsehood of his, it has been already proved, that many other things had been written in the *Gaelic* language. It is not, therefore, likely, that a people so tenacious of their ancestry should leave the histories of their
descent

descent unrecorded. But to presumptive, I shall add positive proof.

I have just now in my possession very complete genealogical accounts of six different families, *viz.* that of the Royal House of *Stuart,* the family of *Argyle, Macdonald,* Mac Ian of *Glenco,* Macneil of *Barra,* and the Bard *Macvurich.* They are all written in the *Gaelic* language and character; and as a proof that they have subsisted for a considerable length of time, it may be proper to inform the Doctor, that the last person mentioned in the second of these genealogies is Archibald earl of Argyle, who succeeded his father in 1661.

I could appeal to many others of very ancient dates; but this much will be sufficient as an answer to our traveller's equally *modest* and *well-founded* assertion, that " no *Earse* genealogy was ever written." I shall

shall not, therefore, trouble the public with a catalogue, which appears unnecessary. There is enough to satisfy the candid; and nothing, I know, will convince the captious. But should any one be still disposed to pay less regard to my private testimony, than to that of Dr. *Johnson*, he may be completely satisfied by applying, in any manner he pleases, to the heads of the families I have mentioned, or to any gentleman or clergyman in the country at large.

It will not, I hope, appear now so very " difficult to tell, where the chiefs of the Highlands have found the histories of their descent." But though nothing of this kind had been anciently written in *Gaelic*, a man of less penetration than the Doctor might easily have conceived, that the genealogies of our great families would naturally be preserved by the same means, to

which

which the families of other countries owe the knowledge of their anceſtry; that is, by charters of lands, contracts of marriage, and ſuch other deeds of a public or private nature as were always recorded every where, and connected the chain of family ſucceſſion.

Page 262. " Thus hopeleſs," ſays he, " are all attempts to find any traces of Highland learning. Nor are their primitive cuſtoms and ancient manner of life otherwiſe than very faintly and uncertainly remembered by the preſent race."

After what has been advanced, *thus hopeleſs* too, I truſt, are all his malignant and impotent attempts to deſtroy either the reality or credit of Highland learning. The traces of it are not ſo obſcure as not to have been eaſily found, had ſuch a reſearch made any part of his buſineſs. But he never inquired about any monument

of

of our antiquities, among such as were the ablest to inform him. He dreaded to hear disagreeable truths from the better sort; and therefore he either made no inquiries at all, or contented himself with the intelligence of the vulgar.

As to what he says about the " primitive customs and ancient manner of life," his observation is too vague and indefinite, in point of time, to admit of an answer, if it otherwise deserved one. Are the customs and manners of remote times otherwise than very faintly and uncertainly remembered by the present race of *English*? I believe it would puzzle the *omnipotent* genius of the Doctor himself, to give satisfactory accounts of those matters at any period before the Norman conquest of his country, or even for some centuries afterwards. There is a folly in the subject of this remark which challenges our contempt

more

more than a serious reply. If it proves any thing, it is the meanness and malignity of the author's own mind; for it shews, that there is nothing either so absurd or trivial but he lays hold of, to form a ground of calumny against the *Scotch*.

In the same page, he says, "To the servants and dependents that were not domestics (and if an estimate be made from the capacity of any of their old houses which I have seen, their domestics could have been but few) were appropriated certain portions of land for their support. *Macdonald* has a piece of ground yet, called the Bards or Senachies field."

It is evident in this place, that the Doctor estimates the number of the domestics by a very false rule. What now is to be seen of the old houses is generally the principal part only, and sometimes but a portion even of that. Around the castle, which was always referved for the chief's own family, and fome of their moft particular friends, there were feveral fmaller buildings for the accommodation of fuch other branches of the clan as might occafionally happen to be there; and on the outfide of all thefe, were the lodging-houfes of the domeftics.

The traces of thofe exterior buildings are ftill vifible in many places; particularly in the neighbourhood of Lochfinlagan, at Dunivaig in *Ifla*, and at Ardtorinifh in *Morvein*. They were likewife, no doubt, to be feen where the Doctor pretends to have made his obfervations; but he chofe to fupprefs that circumftance, that he might take occafion to diminifh the grandeur of our ancient chieftains, in the number of their domeftics; which was certainly much greater than in the prefent times.

His mentioning a piece of ground, belonging to *Macdonald*, which is ftill called the Bard's or Seannachie's field, furnifhes an argument againft himfelf. He faid fome time ago, that neither Bard nor Seannachie had exifted for feveral centuries; and he 'has faid lately, that primitive cuftoms were but faintly and uncertainly remembered by the prefent race of Highlanders. Now, with all due fubmiffion to the Doctor, I muft beg leave to obferve, that, take it which way he will, the one of thefe affertions muft refute the other. If the former be true, the name of the field gives one clear inftance of their remembering a primitive cuftom; but if the Doctor chufes to abide by the latter, it neceffarily brings the exiftence of Bards and Seannachies nearer to our own times, than he had formerly admitted.

In page 267, Dr. *Johnfon* enters into a kind of difquifition concerning the *Earfe*,

the

the vulgar appellation of the *Gaelic* language. Though he acknowledges that " he understands nothing of it," he pronounces it, upon an authority worse, I suppose, than that of his *horse-hirers*, " the rude speech of a barbarous people." To persons as ignorant of the language, and as prejudiced as the Doctor appears to be, this bold assertion may pass for matter of fact. But those who know the *Earse* or *Gaelic* critically, know that our traveller has as much misrepresented our language as he has done our manners.

I have a slight knowledge, at least, of some ancient languages; I understand a few living tongues; and I can aver for truth, before the world, that the *Gaelic* is as copious as the *Greek,* and not less suitable to poetry than the modern *Italian.* Things of foreign or of late invention, may not, probably, have obtained names in the Gaelic language; but every object of nature, and every inftrument of the common and general arts, has many vocables to exprefs it; fuch as fuit all the elegant variations that either the poet or orator may chufe to make.

To prove the copioufnefs of our tongue, it is fufficient to affure the public, that we have a poetical dialect, as well as one fuitable to profe only, that the one never encroaches on the other; and yet that both are perfectly underftood by the moft illiterate, or, if the Doctor rather chufe the word, the moft *unenlightened* Highlanders.

The chief defect in the *Gaelic* tongue proceeds from that, which is reckoned the greateft beauty in other languages. It has too many vowels and diphthongs, which, though fuitable to poetry, renders the pronunciation lefs diftinct and marked than happens in lefs harmonious and confequently

quently more barbarous tongues. Some ignorant writers of the Gaelic have of late, it is true, briftled over their compofitions with too many confonants; but thefe are generally quiefcent in the beginning and end of words, and are preferved only to mark the Etymon.

" Of the *Earfe* language," fays he, " as I underftand nothing, I cannot fay more than I have been told. It is the rude fpeech of a barbarous people, who had few thoughts to exprefs, and were content, as they conceived grofsly, to be grofsly underftood." If the Doctor was ever told what he has here afferted, it muft have been by fome perfon as ignorant of the language as he profeffes himfelf to be, and confequently fuch authority can carry no weight. That a Highlander, who could be the only judge of the matter, fhould have paffed fo unfavourable a verdict on his own language and countrymen, as to call the one a rude fpeech, speech, and the other a barbarous people, is improbable to the last degree. We must suppose, therefore, that our traveller was never told so, or that his informer was an ignorant and presumptuous blockhead.

It will not easily be believed, that the *Gaelic*, which was the language of the *Celtic* nations, can be so very *rude a speech* as the Doctor represents it; or that a powerful people, who extended their dominion over all the countries between *Cape Finisterre* and the mouth of the river *Oby*, could be so very *barbarous*, and have so *few* thoughts to express. Conquest generally civilizes either the victors or the vanquished. It is of no consequence to inquire, what were the manners of our *Celtic* ancestors before they left their native homes. One thing is evident,—that, after mingling with other nations, there appears no reason why their *Scotch* descendants should be more barbarous than their other tribes.

In every country the public as well as private business of a people must be transacted in their native language; and that, by degrees, will improve it into elegance. I know of no instance to the contrary, except in England after the Norman conquest; where, for many centuries, the inhabitants were obliged to learn the language, and to be governed by the laws of their French invaders. Many of their legal *forms* and *phrases*, as well as of their national customs, are still French. In particular, the ceremony of passing bills in parliament is the same with that which was introduced by their foreign lords; and the *nightly* toll of the *curfew* is an everlasting but *mournful* monument of Norman despotism and English subjugation.

These circumstances, no doubt, contributed greatly to retard the improvement of the English language; and accordingly we find, that it was long thought, as Dr. *Johnson*

Johnson expresses it, but a " rude speech" even by the natives themselves; for their best authors, till of very late, wrote always in Latin.

The *Gaelic* was formerly the general language of all Europe. In Scotland it was long the common language, not only of the whole country, but likewise of the court. All the pleadings in the courts of justice, as well as in parliament, were anciently in Gaelic; and we have undoubted testimonies, that even so very lately as in the parliament held at Ardchattan in Argyleshire, in the reign of the great *Robert Bruce*, it was the language in which all their debates were carried on.

It cannot surely appear, from these circumstances, that the *Gaelic* was formerly an uncultivated tongue. If it has not received much improvement of late years, I am certain it has lost little of what it had. It is still the language of a large tract of country;

country; and there are many who write it with elegance and correctness.

This, I think, is as little an evidence of the *Earse* or *Gaelic* being at present a " *rude speech,*" as the Doctor's frequent encomiums on individuals are proofs of a " *barbarous people.*"

But as it was a custom with the Greek and Roman authors to call every thing rude and barbarous which did not belong to themselves, our traveller, perhaps, may think himself entitled to take an equal liberty with whatever is not *English*. If the greatest admirers of the ancients, however, cannot altogether acquit them of illiberality in that mode of speaking, how shall we be able to find an excuse for Dr. *Johnson* in aspiring to the same privilege? The great inferiority of *his* pretensions heightens the offence; and what was only blameable in them,

them, becomes in him a ridiculous and unpardonable prefumption.

" After what has been lately talked," continues he in the fame page, " of Highland Bards, and Highland genius, many will ftartle when they are told, that the *Earfe* never was a written language; that there is not in the world an Earfe manufcript a hundred years old; and that the founds of the Highlanders were never expreffed by letters, till fome little books of piety were tranflated, and a metrical verfion of the Pfalms was made by the fynod of *Argyle*."

As we have nothing here but repetitions of former affertions, the whole of this paffage might be difmiffed, as having been refuted in other places. But I fhall add a few things more, in confirmation of what has been already faid.

That

That not only poems of confiderable length, but likewife genealogies of families, and treatifes on different fubjects, have been anciently written in the *Gaelic*, has been proved by a variety of inftances. Let me now produce an additional teftimony from Mr. Innes. In page 603 of his Inquiry, he mentions a chronicle of a few of our kings, from *Kenneth Macalpine* to Kenneth the Third, fon to Malcolm the Firft; and he fays, that the original chronicle or hiftory, from which that piece was extracted, feems evidently to have been written in the *Gaelic* language, and that fome time too before the year 1291. He has preferved, in his Appendix, the Latin chronicle, which is a copy of the original.

Befides the manufcripts already taken notice of, I could mention many more, were it neceffary, in this place, to trouble the

the reader with a longer list; and other gentlemen are acquainted with a still greater number than has come within my knowledge. Those that yet remain afford more than a presumptive proof, that there once must have been more. I have already pointed out the means, by which most of them were either destroyed or carried away; and even of such as are preserved, many, no doubt, are little heard of, by having fallen into hands that are ignorant of their contents.

From the many accidents, therefore, to which old manuscripts are liable, it would be an unfair way of reasoning to say, that because they are not always to be seen, or because every one is not acquainted with them, they never had existed; and yet this is the very ground upon which Dr. *Johnson* proceeds. If the first person he chanced to interrogate did not say that he had seen the *Gaelic* original of this or that particular subject,

subject, he inquired no further, but immediately set it down as a fact, that no body else had ever seen it, and that no such manuscript had ever existed.

At other times when he met with more intelligent people, who offered to direct him to old manuscripts, he would not suffer himself to be convinced that any such things existed; and if they continued to assert the fact, he generally broke out into an unmannerly rage, declaring, with great vehemence, that if there were any manuscripts in the Highlands, they could not be *Gaelic*, but must certainly be *Irish*.

Thus does Dr. *Johnson* attempt to disprove all traces of Highland learning, by a twofold kind of method; by resting satisfied, in his inquiry, with the answers of the ignorant; and rejecting the assistance of such as were better able to inform him.

His second assertion says, " that there is not in the world an Earse manuscript a hundred years old." This is sufficiently refuted by the dates I have already mentioned, none of which are later than the year 1630; which of itself alone, were there none of a higher antiquity, is enough to put our author to silence, if not to shame.

Among the old MSS. of considerable length, I took notice particularly of two. One gives the history of *Smerbie More*, one of the ancestors of the Duke of Argyle, who lived in the fifth century, according to a MS. genealogy of that illustrious family; and the other contains the history of the sons of *Usnoth*. They are both in the *Gaelic* language and character, and are so very old as to be difficult to be read. They are in the possession of Mr. *Macintyre* of Glenoe, near Bunaw in Argyleshire.

But

But as the Doctor may think it too great a trouble to travel again to the Highlands for a fight of old manuscripts, I shall put him upon a way of being satisfied nearer home. If he will but call some morning on *John Mackenzie*, Esq; of the Temple, Secretary to the Highland Society at the Shakespeare, Covent-Garden, he will find in London more volumes in the *Gaelic* language and character than perhaps he will be pleased to look at, after what he has said. They are written on vellum in a very elegant manner; and they all bear very high marks of antiquity. None of them are of so modern an origin as that mentioned by the Doctor. Some have been written more than five hundred years ago; and others are so very old, that their dates can only be guessed at, from the subjects of which they treat.

Among

Among these are two volumes which are very remarkable. The one is a large folio MS. called *An Duanaireadh Ruadh*, or the *Red rhymer*, which was given by Mr. Macdonald of Glencalladel in *Muideart* to Mr. Macdonald of Kyles in *Cnoideart*, who gave it to Mr. Macpherson. It contains a variety of subjects, such as some of *Ossian*'s Poems, Highland Tales, &c.—The other is called *An Leabhar Dearg*, or the *Red Book*, which was given to Mr. Macpherson by the Bard *Macvurich*. This was reckoned one of the most valuable MSS. in the Bard's possession.

Since I began these Remarks, I have been informed by Mr. Macdonald, the publisher of the *Gaelic* poetry, that his uncle, Mr. Lachlan Macdonald in *South-Uist*, was well acquainted with the last of these manuscripts; and as that gentleman is a great master of the Gaelic language and character, his opinion concerning its antiquity, from the character and other circumstances, is the more to be relied upon.

To finish this head at present, let me next inform the Doctor, that the Bard *Macvurich* alone is in possession of a greater number of *Gaelic* manuscripts than the Doctor perhaps would choose to read in any language. At the earnest and repeated request of Mr. *Macdonald*, the publisher just mentioned, the Bard has been at last prevailed upon to open his repositories, and to permit a part of them to be carried to *Edinburgh*, for the satisfaction of the curious, and the conviction of the incredulous. I myself have seen more than a *thousand* pages of what has been thus obtained, as have hundreds besides; and Mr. *Macdonald* assures me, that what he has got leave to carry away, bears but a very small proportion to what still remains with the Bard.

It seems almost unnecessary to mention that all those manuscripts are in the *Gaelic* language and character. Some of them have suffered greatly by bad keeping; but many more by the ravages of time. The character of several is allowed by all, who have seen the manuscripts, to be the most beautiful they had ever beheld.

From all this, let the public judge of the truth of the Doctor's third assertion in the last cited paragraph, " That the sounds of the Highlanders were never expressed by letters till some little books of piety were translated, and a metrical version of the Psalms was made by the synod of *Argyle.*"

Had he made the proper inquiries, he would have found that Mr. *Robert Kirk*, minister

minister of *Balquidder* in Perthshire, had wrote a *metrical version* of the Psalms prior to that of the synod of *Argyle*. The same gentleman likewise wrote a *Gaelic* Vocabulary, which is mentioned, I think, in *Lhuyd*'s Archæologia Britannica; and from which I have some extracts. But long before all this, there was published a *Gaelic* Treatise on Religion by Bishop *Carswell* of Argyle.

More instances might be given; but these, or any one of them indeed, must as effectually destroy the veracity of the Doctor's assertion, as if a hundred had been produced.

Though it has already appeared that much has been written in the *Gaelic*, and there has, no doubt, been much more than we are now able to discover, I am ready to admit that an equal proportion has not been printed in that language, as in most others.

others. That, however, is easily accounted for. Before publishing in vernacular languages was much used in Europe, the Royal House of *Scotland* had succeeded to the crown of *England*. That event naturally induced men either of ambition or genius to repair to the seat of government, and rendered a more general cultivation of the English language necessary. As therefore every person of any note in the Highlands understood the English perfectly, there could be no great encouragement for many publications in another language, which the poorer sort only had occasion to purchase. Besides, as I observed before, it was thought at one time good policy to suppress the *Gaelic*, though afterwards it has appeared to be a very bad one.

In the same page, our author proceeds, " Whoever therefore now writes in this language, spells according to his own perception

ception of the sounds, and his own idea of the power of the letters. The *Welch* and the *Irish* are cultivated tongues. The Welch, two hundred years ago, insulted their *English* neighbours for the instability of their orthography; while the *Earse* merely floated in the breath of the people, and could therefore receive little improvement."

Nothing can be more false than what is here said of the uncertainty of *Gaelic* orthography. It has a regular and established standard, as is well known to many gentlemen of taste, candour, and curiosity, who, though not natives of the Highlands, have been at much pains to become acquainted with our language. I shall only appeal to two respectable evidences, namely, General Sir *Adolphus Oughton* and Sir *James Foulis*. These gentlemen will give a very different account of the matter from that which is exhibited by Dr. *Johnson*; and yet they cannot be suspected of any national partiality for the *Gaelic*, as Sir *Adolphus* is an *Englishman*, and Sir *James* a South-country *Scot*.

This much, together with the proofs already given of so many manuscripts, treatises, and books in the *Gaelic* language, is sufficient to shew what truth is in the Doctor's assertion, that our language has merely floated in the breath of the people. It would be unnecessary, therefore, to enlarge upon this branch of his doctrine.

In allowing the *Welch* and *Irish* to be cultivated tongues, our author seems not aware that he is paying an indirect compliment to the *Gaelic* at the same time. The Welch has ever been acknowledged to be a dialect of the Celtic or Gaelic; and Mr. Lhuyd, a learned and worthy Welchman, who travelled over all the Highlands, fays, in a letter of his to Mr. *Rowland*, author of *Mona Antiqua*, and publifhed towards the end of that work, that " about two-thirds of the Scots Gaelic is the fame with the Welch." As to the *Irifh*, it is well known to every proper judge to have a ftill greater affinity to our language; for the *Albion* and *Irifh* Gaelic differ not perhaps fo much from each other as any two dialects of the Greek.

But without meaning to derogate from the *Welch* and *Irifh* languages, I fhould be glad to hear the Doctor explain in what particular fenfe he calls them cultivated tongues. If it is only becaufe they form the common fpeech of their refpective countries, the *Gaelic*, in that refpect, ftands upon an equal footing. I have heard of no memorable hiftories, no fyftems of philofophy or politics, which have been publifhed lished in either of those languages. There are Welch and Irish translations of the Bible, and perhaps of some other small tracts, such as the Doctor calls " little books of piety;" and printing, I believe, has not yet been carried much further in any of them. As therefore the *Gaelic* enjoys all these advantages at least, it seems to have equal pretensions to stability.

Page 269. " That the Bards could not read more than the rest of their countrymen, it is reasonable to suppose; because, if they had read, they could probably have written; and how high their compositions may reasonably be rated, an inquirer may best judge by considering what stores of imagery, what principles of ratiocination, what comprehension of knowledge, and what delicacy of elocution he has known any man attain who cannot read."

Here

Here the Doctor seems determined to go to the root of the matter at once. It was necessary for his design to make the Bards appear incapable of recording their own compositions, by asserting that they could neither read nor write; but as that alone would do but half his business, he resolves to go a *little* further. Among his readers there might be some *saucy* folks, who might take upon them to doubt that the Bards could *always* be so very illiterate, if there was any learning in the country. The least suspicion of this kind would have marred the whole plot; and therefore it became absolutely indispensible, with the next dash of his pen, to make the rest of their countrymen as ignorant as he had made the Bards themselves. As this needs no further comment, I shall leave the Doctor, with all the benefit he can derive from pleading the *law of necessity*, to receive the verdict of the public.

As it has so often appeared that Bards could both read and write, the pompous jargon, which closes the above quotation, cannot apply to them, and consequently is only so much ink spilt. But, though the inference deduced therefrom by no means affects the Bards, there is a fallacy in the reasoning, which deserves to be noticed.

I am as ready to admit the general advantages which result from books, as our *book-compiling* journalist himself; but I cannot agree with him in thinking, that the exercise of the mental powers depends entirely upon their assistance. True genius springs from nature: it is her gift alone: it may be improved by reading, but never can be supplied. Every age and country has furnished instances of men, who, by dint of natural talents alone, have acquired a distinction, which others could never attain

tain with their *loads* of learned lumber. Even the wilds of America have produced orators; and poets have flourished beneath arctic skies. In the harangues of the *Indian*, there have been discovered " principles of ratiocination," and a " delicacy of elocution," that would not disgrace a *Cicero*; and, in the free effusions of the *Scandinavian* muse, there are often " stores of imagery," which would equally enrich and adorn the most laboured compositions of Dr. *Johnson*.

In the same page, our traveller proceeds: " The Bard," says he, " was a barbarian among barbarians, who, knowing nothing himself, lived with others that knew no more."—To know but little is a misfortune; but to know *nothing* is the full measure of misery complete.

At what time the whole country was in this forlorn state of combined ignorance and

and barbarity, is not very eafy to tell. If it was before the eftablifhment of *Iona*, which he extols fo much for learning and virtue, the Doctor, I am afraid, fpeaks from conjecture; for the period is fo very diftant, that he could afcertain but little of the true condition of our anceftors before that time. But if it was afterwards, let me afk him, what becomes now of thofe " benefits of knowledge," and thofe " bleffings of religion," which he allows the clans, in p. 346, to have derived from that luminary of the *Caledonian* regions? That furely was an unprofitable knowledge, which left the people ignorant; and that a feeble religion, under which they ftill remained barbarians.

In page 270, he mentions an illiterate poet lately in the Iflands, who, among other things, had compofed a dialogue, of which he heard a part tranflated by a young lady

in

in *Mull*, and thought it had more meaning than he expected from a man totally uneducated. Though this is but a faint way of acknowledging the merits of the dialogue, the anecdote furnishes one strong objection to his late doctrine, concerning the total incapacity of men who could not read. He seems sensible of this; and, to evade the force of it, he endeavours to account for the fact by telling us, that this man " had some opportunities of knowledge; he lived among a learned people."

This, however, is only changing his object with removing the difficulty; for, as through the whole of his *Journey*, contradiction follows the Doctor like a shadow, in attempting to avoid one absurdity, he here falls plump into another. To derogate from the native genius of *one* poor poet, he now makes the *whole* Islanders a learned people; though, at other times,

to

to give the greater weight to his own misrepresentations, he mentions them in a different language. In particular, we cannot have forgot how he characterises them in p. 256, 257. He there says, they are an illiterate people; that they have neither shame from ignorance, nor pride in knowledge; neither curiosity to inquire, nor vanity to communicate.

He next tells us, that there is an antipathy between our language and literature; and that " no man that has learned only *Earse* is, at this time, able to read."— This antipathy, I believe, exists no where but in the Doctor's brain; and it has been already shewn, that many who had " learned only *Earse*" have, at all times, been able both to read and write. Such people correspond regularly in the *Gaelic* language.

His remarks upon the different dialects of the *Gaelic* seem hardly to merit notice. If that circumstance be a defect, it has been the fate of all languages, even the most polished. The *Greek* had many dialects; and, I believe, there is not a province in *France*, or a county in *England*, at this day, that has not many words and modes of pronunciation which are not well understood in others. The inconveniency, however, has the same remedy in the *Gaelic* as in other languages; there is a written diction, which pervades all dialects, and is understood in every island.

In p. 271, he says, "In an unwritten speech, nothing that is not very short is transmitted from one generation to another. Few have opportunities of hearing a long composition often enough to learn it, or have inclination to repeat it so often as is necessary

neceſſary to retain it; and what is once forgotten is loſt for ever."

Having already given ſo many proofs that the *Gaelic* is not " an unwritten ſpeech," I might ſave myſelf the trouble of any particular remarks upon this paſſage; but as there is ſomething ſpecious in the argument, which might impoſe upon unwary readers, a few collateral obſervations may not be improper.

Though nothing had ever been written in the *Gaelic*, the manners and cuſtoms of the Highlanders were peculiarly adapted for preſerving the various productions in their language. The conſtant practice of recitation, which is not yet altogether diſuſed, gave them " opportunities of hearing a long compoſition often enough to learn it;" and their deſire to amuſe themſelves

selves in the solitudes of hunting, or a pastoral life, as well as to bear their part in social entertainments, gave them " inclination to repeat it as often as was necessary to retain it."

In this manner did the inhabitants of every village and valley supply to themselves the want of the more fashionable amusements of towns and cities, and wear off the winter evenings alternately in each other's houses; and in this manner have many things, " not very short," partly written and partly not written, been " transmitted from one generation to another."

By these means, there was no great danger of any thing being so far forgotten as to be " lost for ever;" for if any *one* person should forget a particular part, there were always *thousands* who remembered the whole. Besides, in poetical compositions,

tions, it is well known that the memory is greatly affifted by the cadence and rhyme; and as to fuch pieces of any length as we have in profe, they are the more eafily retained, as they generally confift of a variety of *epifodes*, depending on each other, and highly adapted to captivate the fancy.

Among the latter kind are our *Tales*, which are, for the moft part, of confiderable length, and bear a great refemblance to the *Arabian Nights Entertainments*. One of thofe, in particular, is long enough to furnifh fubject of amufement for feveral nights running. It is called *Scialachd Choife Ce*, or Cian O Cathan's Tale; and though *Scialachies*, or tellers of tales by profeffion, are not now retained by our great families, as formerly, there are many ftill living, who can repeat it from end to end, very accurately.

This

This cannot appear improbable to those who consider, how much the memory is strengthened and improved by frequent use. When duly and constantly exercised, it is capable of surprising exertions; and we have sometimes read of instances, which amount even to prodigies.

I myself once knew a man, who, I am certain, could repeat no less than 15,000 lines; and there is now living one *poet Macintyre*, who can repeat several thousands. This man is altogether illiterate, though not a despicable poet. Besides remembering many of the compositions of others, and likewise of his own not yet published, he lately dictated, from memory, as many songs, composed by himself, as fill a small volume of 162 pages, and amount to upwards of 4000 lines.

There is no doubt, but, in ages when the Highlanders had fewer avocations than at present, there have been instances of memory among them as far superior to those now mentioned, as they are to *that* of Dr. *Johnson*; whose weakness of retention seems to be so great, that he often forgets in the next page what he has advanced in the preceding.

But, if more seems necessary, I must request the Doctor to call to mind what was said in answer to his attack upon the Poems of Ossian, by *W. Cambrensis*, in the St. James's Chronicle of the 23d of March, 1775. " I presume," says that gentleman, " the Doctor must remember boys at school, who would repeat one or all the Eclogues, or a Georgic of Virgil. I can with truth aver, and what many will affirm, that there are several persons in *Wales*, who can repeat the transactions (however fabulous) of *Arthur* and his *mil-wyr*, i. e. his thousand heroes, which are as long as the

the Poems of Ossian." A little after, he adds, " We have still extant in the same manner, *i. e.* handed down by tradition, some of the poems of *Taliesyn pen Byrdd, i. e.* the Chief of Bards, or Poets, in the *Welch* language, and they not inferior to modern poetry of high estimation. *Taliesyn* flourished in the year 500."

The practice of committing much to memory seems to be very old, and probably was borrowed from the *Druids,* who, as we are assured by authors of credit, were obliged to get 20,000 lines by heart, before they were judged fit to exercise their office; for it was an established maxim among them, never to commit any of their religious tenets to writing. I hope the Doctor will not consider it as an affront, that I have taken the liberty to mention an historical fact, which a man of his *profound erudition* might be supposed to know.

In the same page, he goes on: "I believe there cannot be recovered, in the whole *Earse* language, five hundred lines, of which there is any evidence to prove them a hundred years old. Yet I hear that the father of Ossian boasts of two chests more of ancient poetry, which he suppresses, because they are too good for the *English*."

I shall make no other answer to the first part of this passage, than by referring the reader to the numerous manuscripts, volumes, and dates, which have been already mentioned. As to the anecdote relative to Mr. Macpherson, whom our traveller sarcastically terms the Father of Ossian, I am glad to have it in my power to expose its falsehood, by the most direct and unequivocal proof.

Though I had found so many reasons to doubt the credit of Dr. Johnson's *bare* assertion,

sertion, and though the general character of the gentleman he accuses, rendered it highly improbable that he could have expressed himself in terms so inconsistent with moderation, if not with prudence and good sense, yet I was desirous, in a point so very delicate, to have something positive to produce. As I had not the pleasure of Mr. Macpherson's acquaintance, I requested the favour of one of his friends, to whom I am known, to desire him to give a *true* state of the matter. He was obliging enough to comply; and Mr. Macpherson's answer was nearly in these words:

" Dr. Johnson has either been deceived himself, or he wittingly deceives others. That I might have said in company, that there still remained many poems in my hands *untranslated*, is not improbable, as the fact is true; but that I should have accompanied that assertion with a sarcasm on the English nation, is *impossible*; as I have all along most thoroughly despised and detested those narrow principles, which suggest national reflections to illiberal minds. I have lived in England long; I have met with public favour; I have experienced private friendship; and, I trust, I shall not, like some others, speak disrespectfully of the bulk of a nation, by whom, as individuals, I have been uniformly treated with civility, and from whom I have often received favours. As I never courted the friendship, nor was ambitious of the company, of Dr. Johnson, he cannot authenticate the assertion, from his own knowledge; and if he received the anecdote from others, they either flattered his prejudices, or imposed upon his weakness."

Page 272, he gives such an account of Highland narration, as plainly discovers what sort of people he interrogated. In one

one place, he says, " The inhabitants knowing the ignorance of all strangers in their language and antiquities, perhaps are not very scrupulous adherents to truth." Soon after, he adds, " They have inquired and considered little, and do not always feel their own ignorance. They are not much accustomed to be interrogated by others, and seem never to have thought upon interrogating themselves."

After what we have heard the Doctor say before, in favour of the clergy and better sort of people, it is evident he can here mean only the vulgar. What, then, are we to think of a man who could be weak enough to expect accurate intelligence from that class of the inhabitants, and afterwards be so very disingenuous as to characterise the whole country from *their* measure of knowledge? Their answers, I allow, could not always be satisfactory and juft; but yet, though fuch poor people could have little elfe than the received traditions of the country to affift them, it is fimply impoffible they fhould always be in the wrong. It was when their anfwers came neareft to the truth, that they were moft offenfive to Dr. *Johnfon*. A genuine account of the facts did not fuit his purpofe, and therefore it became neceffary to difparage the teftimony he received. To effect this, a double charge of *ignorance* and *deceit*, in the inhabitants, is made ufe of, though any one of them would have been fufficient. But it has been all along the peculiar misfortune of our traveller to overact his part; fo that by endeavouring to be too fecure, he has often defeated his own views.

To corroborate the above remarks, the Doctor calls in the teftimony of his friend and fellow-traveller. " Mr. Bofwell," continues

continues he, " was very diligent in his inquiries; and the result of his investigations was, that the answer to the second question was commonly such as nullified the answer to the first."

Though Mr. James Boswell was the *fidus Achates* of our " Peregrinator," his attendance and services are seldom " commemorated" in the work now under consideration. The last time he was mentioned, we found him employed in the notable exploit of " catching a cuddy;" now he is brought in by the head and shoulders, as an evidence against Highland narration. This sullen silence of our author, relative to his friend, is but a scurvy kind of behaviour towards a man, who evidently wished, that his *jolly-boat* might be carried down in tow, along the tide of time, by this *first-rate* man of letters.

Mr. Boswell, it seems, has made several attempts to place his own statue in one of the niches in the temple of Fame. He too, like our traveller, wrote " a Journey." In a violent episode in his work, he has introduced his *learned friend* in the character of a legislator among the wilds of *Corsica*. There is more of ridicule, than of applause, in making a man, who has not the least command over his own passions, " the fabricator of a system of polity to an infant state." But I dare say, that Mr. Boswell was serious; and that what some might consider as an injudicious piece of adulation, was actually the result of a fixed admiration of the talents of his literary friend.

The return made by this literary friend is more suitable to his own malevolence, than to his gratitude to Mr. Boswell. That gentleman's polite acquiescence, he has most probably perverted, in this place, to a proof of a fact, which he was resolved,
at

at all events, to eſtabliſh. Mr. Boſwell, it is well known, is as abſolute a ſtranger to what Doctor *Johnſon* calls the Earſe language, as the Doctor himſelf; and, conſequently, the latter might as well have taken his *own* opinion upon the ſubject, as to have called in the aid of his fellow-traveller's teſtimony.

There is, however, a degree of judgment, though none of candour, in the Doctor's conduct upon this occaſion. The ſuppoſed teſtimony of a native, who muſt have had a natural attachment to his own country, could not fail to ſtrengthen the probability of facts, tending to throw diſcredit on Scotland. In this light, even the acquieſcence of Mr. Boſwell was blameable; as he might have perceived the drift of the Doctor's query. Good-nature may be ſometimes carried to an extreme that is culpable. To this weak, though amiable virtue, we are willing to aſcribe Mr. Boſwell's conduct; and not to a deſire of ſacrificing every thing to the prejudices of a literary *Moloch*, whom he seems to have too much worshipped.

Page 273. " We were a while told," says the Doctor, " that they had an old translation of the Scriptures; and told it till it would appear obstinacy to inquire again. Yet by continued accumulation of questions we found, that the translation meant, if any meaning there were, was nothing else than the *Irish* Bible."

When the Doctor acknowledges that he was so repeatedly told of an old translation of the Scriptures in the *Gaelic* language, and at the same time avows his own obstinacy in disbelieving the fact, he gives a striking proof how difficult it was to convince him of any thing in favour of the country. A stubborn incredulity in such circumstances, and a resolution *not* to be persuaded, is one and the same thing. If he he was to reject all testimony, I would beg leave to ask him, in what manner he could propose to be satisfied? He could not surely be absurd enough to imagine, that every person, who mentioned the existence of such a manuscript translation, should be able to prove his assertion, by producing a copy. It was a work of too great length and labour to be looked for in private hands.

That there was such a translation, is beyond all doubt. It was lately in the library of *Archibald* Duke of *Argyle*; and it is still, no doubt, in the possession of his successors. It was never printed, for reasons already observed. Before the two kingdoms fell under the sway of one sovereign, there was little printed any where in vernacular tongues. After that period, a kind of policy was adopted, though since found to be a bad one, for refusing any public encouragement to the *Gaelic* language,

guage, that the lower sort of people in the Highlands might be under a necessity of learning the *English*. The intention was, to abolish the chief national distinction between the inhabitants of both kingdoms, and assimilate them more to each other, by an uniformity of speech. This, for a long time, prevented any publication of consequence from appearing in our language. But the error has been at length discovered; and now the *Gaelic*, by degrees, has begun to find employment for the press.

With regard to the other portions of Scripture, I shall refer the Doctor to Mr. *Pennant*'s Tour in 1769. In page 134 of the Appendix, he will find, that " *Gilbert Murray* archdeacon, afterwards bishop of Murray, translated the Psalms and Gospels into the *Irish* language and *Scots* Gaelic, in the 12th century." He may here observe, that the Irish language and the
Scots

Scots Gaelic are ufed as fynonymous terms. This, I have already taken notice, is a very improper way of fpeaking; but as it has been fometimes a' practice, on account of the very inconfiderable difference between thefe two dialects of the ancient *Celtic*, to exprefs the one by the other, it is fufficient to deftroy the effect intended by our traveller, from the authority of *Martin*, in the following paffage.

" We heard," he goes on, " of manufcripts that were, or that had been in the hands of fomebody's father, or grandfather; but at laft we had no reafon to believe they were other than Irifh. Martin mentions Irifh, but never any Earfe manufcripts, to be found in the iflands in his time."

The Doctor repeats the fame thing fo often, that, in following him through the progrefs of his *Journey*, I find myfelf likewife led into tautologies, for which I muſt beg the reader's indulgence.

Had he inquired of the proper people, he would not have heard ſuch a vague account of manuſcripts, as that they only " were, or had been in the hands of ſomebody's father, or grandfather." He would have met with gentlemen, who could have ſhewn him there were manuſcripts in their *own* hands; and that they had been tranſmitted in their families, through the *hands* of a long ſeries of *forefathers*. But the laugh, which the Doctor means to excite, by this mode of expreſſion, is loſt in the improbability of the fact which he relates. We behold, therefore, the harmleſs but pitiful trick of an *old* man, who hopes, but without effect, to cheat his reader into the belief of a fiction, by an attempt to put him firſt in good humour.

Though

Though the manuscripts I have already mentioned are sufficient to establish the antiquity, as well as the great diversity of writing in the *Gaelic* language, I shall here add a few observations more; and hope it will be the last time I shall have occasion to resume any discussion on the same subject.

There are still many other manuscripts in the Highlands, both in verse and prose, which are of great antiquity, and of which I shall take notice only of a few.

Among the former, in particular are, a poem called *Côachac na Sróna*, and the *Aged Bard's Wish*, both of which have been lately published. These, with a variety of others, seem to go as far back as the ages of hunting; for they contain not the smallest allusion to agriculture, or any of the modern arts of life. Among other circumstances of a very ancient nature,

nature, some of them make frequent mention of a species of *deer*, which has been extinct in the Highlands for some centuries; and of which we know nothing now but from these poems, and from their huge heads and horns, which are often dug up in our bogs and mosses. Many will understand, that the creature I mean is the Lŏn; which was probably a species of the elk or moose deer.

But to relieve our peregrinator, at once, from his " *wild-goose chace*" after manuscripts, of which he could *only* learn that they formerly had been in *somebody*'s hands, I will refer him to two gentlemen, who will give him a more positive information. Dr. *Alexander Campbel* in Argyleshire will, among other things, make him acquainted with a very old MS. in *Gaelic* character, which makes a large volume of a quarto size; and which, with a variety

of

of other subjects, gives a particular account of the *feuds* which had formerly subsisted between the families of *Fion* (or Fingal) and *Gaul*.

Dr. *Campbel* is, in every other view, a very respectable character; and his great age, being now upwards of eighty years, has enabled him, in particular, to acquire a very extensive knowledge of the antiquities of his country. He was told by his father, the celebrated Mr. *Colin Campbel* minister of *Ardchattan*, a man eminent for learning in general, and for mathematical and antiquarian knowledge in particular, that the greatest part of the books of value belonging to *Iona*, in the latter centuries, were carried to *Doway* in French *Flanders*; where the *Scots* had a seminary, which still continues. Here the curious will, no doubt, find something worth the trouble of inquiry.

The other gentleman I intend to mention, and who, after the many testimonies already produced, shall be the last authority I will advance on the subject of *Gaelic* manuscripts, is Mr. *Maclachlan* of Kilbride. He has been esteemed, and very deservedly, one of the greatest antiquarians, of his time, in the Highlands; and our traveller will find in his family a variety of *Gaelic* manuscripts and fragments, which have been transmitted, from father to son, for many generations.

As for the antiquity of learning and writing in general, in Scotland, it is universally acknowledged by all nations; and notwithstanding the many misfortunes which have befallen the works of our learned men, there still remain convincing proofs, that we had our full proportion of them in former times. I shall but slightly touch upon a few particulars.

The Doctor will startle, perhaps, when he is told, that *Gildas* was born at *Dunbarton*, which is still the capital of a Highland county.—*Cumineus* and *Adamnanus* were abbots of *Iona*; and besides the Life of St. *Columba*, they wrote other historical treatises. They flourished above eleven hundred years ago; and their writings that remain are sustained as genuine by all the learned in Europe. They wrote before the Saxon historian *Bede*. Could we recover more of what has been anciently written at *Iona*, there is good authority for believing, that we should find the lives, deaths, and chief actions of their kings, who, before the union of the *Scottish* and *Pictish* kingdoms, used to be crowned and buried there, recorded by those and other *religionists* of that renowned seminary.

An author of the 12th century mentions *Scots* records, as then reckoned ancient.

cient. He was cotemporary with *Andrew* bishop of *Caithness*, who died in 1185, and is quoted by *Camden*. This writer, in a description of *Albany*, the ancient name of Scotland, speaks of our histories to this effect. " We read," says he, " in the histories and chronicles of the ancient Britons, and in the ancient atchievements and annals of the Scots and Picts, &c."— This, I presume, will satisfy the most scrupulous, that writings, which could be called ancient by an author of the 12th age, must have been of no short standing.

In the last cited page, " I suppose," says our traveller, " my opinion of the Poems of Ossian is already discovered." Indeed! —There is no need, surely, for a very uncommon degree of penetration to make this discovery. The *cloven foot* has appeared long ago; and a man must be very dull, who could not perceive which way it it pointed. To render the authenticity of those poems suspicious, was the great object of his *Journey*; and to facilitate the execution of that project, has he *toiled* so much before-hand in discrediting Highland learning and narration. How far he has succeeded in the preparatory part, the public will judge from what has gone before; with what effect he now makes a more direct attack upon the poems themselves, will appear from what follows.

I shall only premise, that I will not here, as on other occasions, quote the particular objections of our traveller, and answer them one by one; but continue the thread of observation, without any interruption, and with as little personal application as possible. The malignity of a few others, the prejudices of several, and the weakness of many have suggested similar objections to the authenticity of *Ossian*'s

Poems,

Poems, which have lately come to my hands. I shall therefore endeavour to obviate the whole upon the same general ground.

The concurrent testimony of a whole people, and the evidence of many respectable individuals, laid before the public by that elegant writer and respectable clergyman, Dr. *Blair*, have been found incapable, it seems, to satisfy the minds of men, who are unwilling to give credit to any thing calculated to reflect honour on the ancestors of the *Scotch* nation. To persuade such men of the truth of any fact, which they are resolved *not* to believe, is beyond my wish, as well as my expectation. But as many candid and well-meaning persons have been seduced into an error, by the bold assertions of the prejudiced and incredulous, I shall examine, in a succinct manner, the objections on which they found their want of faith.

Some

Some derive an objection to the authenticity of *Offian*'s Poems, from an alleged superciliousness in Mr. *Macpherson*, in refusing satisfaction, on that head, to every writer, with or without a name, who chooses to demand that satisfaction, at the bar of the public. Though I am told that superciliousness is no part of Mr. *Macpherson*'s character, I think he has a right to assume it on such occasions. To answer the queries of the prejudiced would have no effect; and there can be no end to solving the difficulties started by the ignorant. The most loud and clamorous are generally those who are least entitled to satisfaction; and were Mr. *Macpherson* to descend into a controversy, upon a mere matter of fact, he would, in a manner, leave truth to the decision of sophistry.

Mr. *Macpherson* has done all that could, or ought to be expected. He has never refused

refused the examination or perusal of his manuscripts to persons of taste and knowledge in the *Celtic* language. These are the best, if not the only judges of the subject; and as these are perfectly satisfied as to the authenticity of the poems, Mr. *Macpherson* has a right to be totally indifferent to the incredulity of others.

To extend the opportunity of judging for themselves, to such as are conversant in the language of the ancient *Scots*, and yet have no opportunity of examining Mr. *Macpherson*'s originals, he has published the seventh Book of *Temora*. He went further. He published proposals for printing *all* the poems by subscription; but, as no subscribers appeared, he justly took it as the sense of the public, that the authenticity, as being a matter of such general notoriety, was absolutely and decisively admitted.

The

The specimen, which the translator has published, carries to my mind, and, I trust, I have some right to form a judgment on such subjects, a thorough conviction, that the seventh Book of *Temora* is not of Mr. *Macpherson*'s composition. If it had been of his own composition, how could he mistake the meaning of a passage in it, as it is evident he has done? To every Highlander, to every man of candour in any country, this is a decisive proof of the authenticity of the poems. Neither the bold assertions of the prejudiced, nor all the sophistry of criticism, can persuade the world, that any man can mistake the meaning of what he has written himself.

But though the Poems of *Ossian* bear every internal mark of originality, though they convey no ideas, exhibit no ornaments, contain no sentiments, which are not peculiarly *Celtic*, according to the accounts

counts we have received of Celtic manners from the ancients, WE, the natives of the Highlands, and *we* certainly muſt be allowed to be the beſt judges of the matter, do not found their authenticity on internal proofs. Every man of inquiry, every perſon of the leaſt taſte for the poetry, or turn for the antiquities of his country, has heard often repeated ſome part or other of the poems publiſhed by Mr. *Macpherſon*. Hundreds ſtill alive have heard portions of them recited, long before Mr. *Macpherſon* was born; ſo that he cannot poſſibly be deemed the author of compoſitions, which exiſted before he had any exiſtence himſelf.

It is true, there is no man now living, and perhaps there never has exiſted any one perſon, who either can or could repeat the whole of the Poems of *Oſſian*. It is enough, that the whole has been repeated, in

[Marginal note:] I have now seen this author's collection. He may have recognised part of it in MacPherson's Purloph. but there is not one line of the Gaelic of 1807 in his [original?] collection so far as I have been able to find out. J. Campbell. 9th Feby 1871. Brebst [?]

in detached pieces, through the Highlands and Isles. Mr. *Macpherson's* great merit has been the collecting the *disjecta membra poetæ*; and his fitting the parts so well together, as to form a complete figure. Even the perfect symmetry of that figure has been produced, as an argument against its antiquity. But arguments are lost, and facts are thrown away, upon men, who have *predetermined* to resist conviction itself.

In vain has it been alleged, that the age of hunting, in which the *Fingalians* are said to have lived, cannot be supposed to have cultivated poetry. This objection is started by men, who are more acquainted with books than human nature. But had they even consulted their books, they might have received a complete answer to their objection. The *Scandinavians*, who lived in a country almost as unsit for

pasture

pasture as for the plough, excelled in the beautiful and sublime of poetry. Their war songs, their funeral elegies, their love sonnets, convey more exalted ideas of magnanimity, melancholy, and tenderness, than the most laboured compositions of Greece and Rome, on the same subjects. The allusions are few and simple; but they are calculated to impress the mind with that " glow of feeling," which springs only from genuine poetry.

Are the *Indians* of America any more than mere hunters? Yet who can deny them a claim to the possession of poetry? Their whole language seems to be, as it were, *infected* with poetical metaphor. Their orations at their Congresses, upon matters of business, are all in the poetical style. They resemble more the speeches in the *Iliad*, than those dry syllogistical disquisitions, which have banished all the beautiful

beautiful simplicity of eloquence from modern public assemblies.

Besides, is there any person acquainted with the natives of the Highlands, who does not know, that such persons as are most addicted to hunting, are most given to poetry? One of the best songs preserved in *Macdonald*'s collection of *Gaelic* poems, is altogether on the subject of hunting, and the date of its composition is so old, that it lies beyond the reach of tradition itself. The solitary life of a hunter is peculiarly adapted to that melancholy, but spirited and magnificent turn of thought, which distinguishes our ancient poetry.

But it is not necessary to consider the *Fingalians* as mere hunters. We frequently find in *Ossian*'s Poems allusions to flocks and herds; and a pastoral life has been universally allowed to have been

A a peculiarly

peculiarly favourable to the muse. I could never see, for my own part, any reason for supposing that agriculture itself was unknown in the days of *Ossian*, though it is not mentioned in his poems. With a contempt for every thing but the honour acquired by the sword, he perhaps considered the plough as too mean an instrument to be alluded to in compositions chiefly intended to animate the soul to war.

The dignified sentiments, the exalted manners, the humanity, moderation, generosity, gallantry, and tenderness for the fair sex, which are so conspicuous in the Poems of *Ossian*, have been brought as arguments against their authenticity. These objections, however, proceed either from an ignorance of history, a want of knowledge of human nature, or those confined notions concerning the character of ages and

and nations, which are too often entertained in certain univerſities. With the literature of Greece and Rome, they imbibe ſuch an exalted idea of claſſic character, as induces them to conſign to ignorance and barbariſm, all antiquity beyond the pales of the Greek and Roman empires.

But had they conſulted the hiſtory of other nations, they might find that the want of refinement, which is called barbariſm, does not abſolutely prove the want of noble and generous qualities of the mind. The powers of the ſoul are in every country the ſame. Why then ſhould not the Celtic *Druid* be as capable of impreſſing uſeful inſtruction on the followers of his religion, as the bare-footed *Selli* *,

---

* The *Selli* were certainly as unpoliſhed as any *Druid*, in the moſt barbarous and ſequeſtred parts of the Highlands and *Scottiſh* Iſles.

———— Ἀμφὶ δὲ Σελλοὶ
Σ) ναιυ<unclear>,</unclear> ἑμφῆται ἀνιπτόποδες, χαμαιεῦναι.

Iliad xvi. v. 234, 235.

who sacrificed to *Jupiter* on the cold top of *Dodona*? Or, by what prescription has the neighbourhood of the *Hellespont* a right to sentiments more exalted than those of the chieftain who inhabits the coast of the *Vergivian* ocean? Have not many nations, who have been called barbarians, excelled the Romans in valour, and in that most exalted of all virtues, a sincere love for their country?

Have not even the *Canadians* of North America, with fewer opportunities of improvement than the *Fingalians*, been found to possess almost all the virtues celebrated in the Poems of *Ossian* *? Why therefore should we deny to the ancient *Caledonians* what we cannot refuse to the modern neighbours of the *Eskimaux*?

The truth is, that the resemblance at least, of all the virtues contained in the

* Abbé de Raynal, tom. iv.

Poems of *Ossian*, and which are probably exaggerated in the usual manner of poetry, still remains in the Highlands of Scotland. The valour of the *Highlanders* is allowed by their greatest enemies; and the most prejudiced cannot accuse them of cruelty. Battle seems always to have been more their object, than the rewards of victory. In the social virtues, the lowest Highlander is not, even in this age, deficient. He is civil, attentive, and hospitable to strangers, in a degree unknown in any other country; and as to matrimonial fidelity and attachment, and delicacy towards women, the Highlanders are exceeded by none; I mean such of them as have not *improved* their manners into a neglect of *trivial* virtues, by a frequent intercourse with Dr. *Johnson*'s countrymen.

In ancient times, the Highlanders had much better opportunities to learn exalted

sentiments, if such *must* be learnt, than in later ages. The most prejudiced of our opponents will allow, that refinement is in every country, in a certain degree, an inseparable appendage of a court. In the days of *Fingal*, and for many ages after him, the Highlands were the seat of government. After the extinction, or rather the conquest of the *Picts*, the kings of the Scots fixed their residence in the low country. When the southern parts of Scotland were wrested from the *Saxons* and *Danes*, an extension of territory and the danger of a southern enemy carried the seat of government still further from the Highlanders. This circumstance had certainly its weight in depriving the posterity of the *Fingalians* of some part of that exalted character, which distinguished their ancestors. But their retaining still so many of the virtues celebrated by *Ossian*, is certainly a good argument, that those
virtues

virtues might have exifted in their perfection, in more favourable times.

But there is little occafion for fpeculative reafoning on a matter which is fo well eftablifhed by fact. A whole people give their teftimony to the exiftence of the Poems of *Offian*; and gentlemen of the firft reputation for veracity, and a capacity to judge of the fubject, have long ago permitted their names to be given to the public, as vouchers for many parts of the collection publifhed by Mr. *Macpherfon*. Many more are ready to join their teftimony to that already given to the world. The truth is, that even the defending a matter of fuch notoriety, is the moft plaufible argument that the prejudiced could have brought againft the authenticity of the poems.

To put the matter beyond the contradiction of the prejudiced, and the unbelief of the most incredulous, I am glad to be able to inform the public, that the whole of the Poems of *Ossian* are speedily to be printed in the original *Gaelic*. In vain will it be said by Dr. *Johnson* and others, who have manifestly *resolved* not to believe the authenticity of the poems, that the same man, who could invent them in English, might clothe them in a *Celtic* dress. To this I answer, that it would be impossible for any person, let his talents be ever so great, to impose a *translation*, for an original, on any critic in the Gaelic language.

Dr. *Johnson* will certainly permit me to ask him, Whether any of his countrymen could imitate the language of the age of *Chaucer*, so as to pass his own work, for a composition of those times? Dr. *Johnson*'s critical knowledge of the English language would spurn the idea; but I will venture to to assure the Doctor, that we have, among us, several persons as conversant in the old Gaelic, as he himself is in the tongue of the ancient Saxons.

In the arrangement of the whole work, and even in the improvement of particular passages, the public are perhaps indebted to the taste and judgment of Mr. *Macpherson*. Being perfectly master of all the traditions relative to the *Fingalian* times, he has, no doubt, availed himself of that advantage, in placing the poems in their most natural order; and in restoring the scattered members of such pieces, as he found floating on tradition only, to their original stations. As he collected some parts of the poems from what Dr. *Johnson* would call the " recitation of the aged," in different parts of the country, he was certainly excusable in taking the " best readings in all the editions," if the expression may be used.

Thus

Thus far we will admit, that Mr. Macpherson is the *author* of the poems. But more we will neither grant to him, nor to Dr. *Johnson*; who seems not to be aware of the compliment he pays to a writer, who, by meriting his envy, has excited his malevolence.

It has upon the whole appeared, that the knowledge of letters was introduced into the *Highlands* and *Hebrides*, in as early a period of time as into any of the neighbouring countries. That one of the first uses made of those letters was the recording of works of genius, as well as public events. That, as a collateral security for handing down the compositions of the poet, as well as the facts related by the historian, there were *Bards* and *Seanachies*, educated in academies, and retained afterwards by the principal families in the Highlands and Isles. That those Bards and Seanachies were not an illiterate race

of

of men, apt to corrupt poetry and miſtake facts. That both of them could, and actually did, write the *Gaelic* language, without receiving their knowledge of letters through the *medium* of any other tongue. That the Bards and Scanachies were ſo far from becoming extinct ſome centuries ago, that a few of them ſtill exiſt. That, beſides the regular and retained Bards and Seanachies, there were many other perſons, who executed the duties of their offices, through a particular turn of genius, or an attachment to the antiquities and poetry of their country. That of theſe ſeveral ſtill exiſt; and many more were exiſting a few years ago. That the buſineſs of the eſtabliſhed Bards and Scanachies, as well as of thoſe who followed the profeſſions of both through pleaſure, was to tranſmit poetry and hiſtory to poſterity, ſometimes by writing, but oftener by oral tradition. That the Poems of *Oſſian* have been handed down

down by thefe means, from age to age, to the prefent times. That, in old times, no doubt of their authenticity was ever entertained; and that there are ſtill exiſting many hundreds, nay many thouſands, who are ready to atteſt their coming down to them, from antiquity, with all the proofs neceſſary to eſtabliſh an indubitable fact.

The Doctor concludes his obſervations on the Poems of *Oſſian*, by paſſing two very ſevere reflections; the one of a perſonal, the other of a national kind. As what he ſays is pretty remarkable, I ſhall give it in his own words.

" I have yet," ſays he, " ſuppoſed no impoſture but in the publiſher;" and, a little after, he adds, " The Scots have ſomething to plead for their eaſy reception of an improbable fiction: they are ſeduced by their fondneſs for their ſuppoſed anceſtors. A Scotchman muſt be a very

ſturdy

sturdy moralist, who does not love *Scotland* better than truth; he will always love it better than inquiry; and, if falsehood flatters his vanity, will not be very diligent to detect it."

As an imposture is the last thing of which a gentleman can be supposed guilty, it is the last thing with which he ought to be charged. To bring forward such an accusation, therefore, without proof to establish it, is a *ruffian* mode of impeachment, which seems to have been reserved for Dr. *Johnson*. There is nothing in his " *Journey to the Hebrides*" to support so gross a calumny, unless we admit his own *bare* assertions for arguments; and the publisher, if by the publisher he means Mr. *Macpherson*, is certainly as incapable of an imposture, as the Doctor is of candour or good manners.

The indelicacy of such language is obvious. A gentleman would not have expressed himself in that manner, for his own sake; a man of prudence would not have done it, for fear of giving just offence to Mr. Macpherson. But the Doctor seems to have been careless about the reputation of the first of those characters; and the malignity of his disposition seems to have made him overlook the foresight generally annexed to the second. Though he was bold in his assertions, however, I do not find he has been equally courageous in their defence. His mere allegation on a subject which he could not possibly understand, was unworthy of the notice of the gentleman accused; but the language, in which he expressed his doubts, deserved chastisement. To prevent this, he had age and infirmities to plead; but not content with that security, which, I dare venture to say, was sufficient, he declared, when queftioned, that he would call the laws of his country to his aid. Men, who make a breach upon the laws of good manners, have but a fcurvy claim to the protection of any other laws.

Nor will our traveller come better off with the public, in his more general affault. No man, whofe opinion is worth the regarding, will give credit to fo indifcriminate a calumny: the Doctor, therefore, has exhibited this fpecimen of his rancour to no other purpofe, than either to gratify the prejudiced, or to impofe upon the weak and credulous. If any thing can be inferred from what he fays, it is only this, that he himfelf is not fo " very fturdy a moralift" as to love *truth* fo much as he hates *Scotland*.

Soon after this, he tells us, that he left *Sky* to vifit fome other iflands. But as

his

his obfervations, through that part of his *Journey*, prefent nothing new, I fhall not follow him in his progrefs; and the reader, I believe, as well as myfelf, will have no objection to be relieved, from his long attendance on fo uncouth a companion. We fhall leave him, therefore, to rail, in the old way, at the poverty, ignorance, and barbarity of the inhabitants; while, with a peculiar confiftency, he acknowledges plenty, intelligence, and politenefs, every where. Neither fhall we difturb his meditations among the ruins of *Iona*; but permit him to tread that *once* hallowed fpot with reverential awe, and demonftrate the *true* fpirit of his faith, by mourning over the " dilapidated monuments of ancient fanctity."

When he tells us, page 376, that men bred in the univerfities of *Scotland* obtain only a mediocrity of knowledge between

learning

learning and ignorance, he contradicts his own attestations to the contrary in a thousand different places. I formerly compared this passage with his *elogiums* on the Highland clergy; I must now contrast it with what he mentions in two or three pages after. " We now," says he, " returned to *Edinburgh*, where I passed some days with men of learning, whose names want no advancement from my commemoration." It was somewhat careless in the Doctor, to say no worse, to hold so very different a language in page 379, while the censure passed on our universities, but so little before, must be recent in the reader's memory. But a regard to the *trifling* forms of consistency seems never to have been an object of his attention.

It happens luckily, however, that the reputation of the *Scots* for learning rests upon a better foundation than the opinion of Dr. *Johnson*. The testimony of the world is in their favour; and, against that, *his* praise or censure can have but little weight. The three learned professions bear witness to their knowledge and talents. In physic they stand unrivalled; and in the pulpit and at the bar they have no superiors.

But, besides professional merit, the Scots have long occupied every other department of literature; and they have distinguished themselves in each. The province of history is, in a manner, yielded up to them; they have added largely to the various stores of philosophy and the mathematics; and, in criticism and the *belles lettres*, they have discovered abilities, and acquired applause. Though they seldom descend to the *ludicrous*, yet they have not wanted writers, who have made some figure in that walk. If the Doctor doubts the fact, I shall

shall refer him, for information, to the author of *Lexiphanes*.

I shall now take a final leave of Dr. Johnson. That he set out with an intention to traduce the *Scots* nation, is evident; and the account he gives of his Journey shews, with what a stubborn malignity he persevered in that purpose. Every line is marked with prejudice; and every sentence teems with the most illiberal invectives. If he has met with some correction, in the course of this examination, it is no more than he ought to have expected; unless he feels in his own mind, what his pride perhaps will not allow him to acknowledge, that misrepresentation and abuse merit no passion superior to contempt.

FINIS.

ERRATA.

Page 4. line 1. *for* about two years *read* some years.
  ib. —— 20. *for* on *read* to.
  7. —— 9. *for* Gallic *read* Gaelic.
  18. —— 10. *for* of *read* on.
  39. —— 16. *for* no authority *read* no synonimous authority.
  50. —— ult. *for* Introducing *read* In traducing.
  57. —— 15. *for* Follafandus *read* Fullofaudes.
  71. —— 5. *for* Gallic *read* Gaelic.
  74. —— 18. *for* Gallic *read* Gaelic.

www.ingramcontent.com/pod-product-compliance
Lightning Source LLC
Chambersburg PA
CBHW030357230426
43664CB00007BB/636